Word of Life

MARTIN KITCHEN is a graduate in modern languages and theology of the University of London and holds a doctorate in New Testament Studies from the University of Manchester. He prepared for ordination at King's College, London, and with the Southwark Ordination Course and is a Residentiary Canon of Durham Cathedral.

GEORGIANA HESKINS is Tutor at the South East Institute for Theological Education where she teaches Pastoral and Biblical Studies. She is a priest-vicar at Southwark Cathedral and lives in south east London. Her preparation for ordination was at King's College, London, and at Wescott House in Cambridge and most of her preaching experience was gained in London.

STEPHEN MOTYER spent some years at the pulpit-face trying to make the lectionary live in rural Hertfordshire, before taking up his present post as New Testament Lecturer at London Bible College. Before that he taught at Oak Hill College, and looks back with thankfulness on theological studies at Cambridge, Bristol, Tübingen and London. With the other authors of this Commentary, he shares a vision for inspiring preaching at the heart of worship.

Contents

Foreword

How should the Word of God be read in public worship? In one sense, it is obvious that certain gospel passages are winners at Christmas and Easter; and we all have our favourites here and there. But it did not take the Church long to discover the need for some kind of basic order. So lectionaries developed, and a certain centralization took over in the East and West.

By far the most significant development of modern times was the scheme approved by the Roman Catholic Church in 1969, the fruit of important collaboration between biblical scholars and liturgists. It was soon seized upon in North America and adapted to the needs of other churches: Anglican, Lutheran, Presbyterian and Methodist. The *Revised Common Lectionary* of 1992 represents this international, ecumenical reception and adjustment. And it was only going to be a matter of time before the Church of England's General Synod should adopt it – which it did in the summer of 1996.

The most significant change is that the books of the Bible are read – as far as possible – in course, most notably the gospels. Whereas other lectionaries tend to skip from one book to another, the *Revised Common Lectionary* is more settled. For worshippers – preachers included – there is the opportunity for sustained nourishment.

A new lectionary of this kind can only benefit from the depth of elucidation offered here by Martin Kitchen and his two collaborators, Georgiana Heskins and Stephen Motyer. The love for sacred scripture and the easy discernment of which background details are needed shine through in this companion volume.

The *Revised Common Lectionary* is authorized in the Church of England from Advent of 1997, which is 'Year C' in the new scheme. I am sure I am not alone in looking forward to two further volumes to complete the three-year cycle. Those responsible for preparing sermons will find here a wealth of reflection and learning. Let these pages be read and pondered by all whose hearts are intent on celebrating God's Word with understanding.

† KENNETH PORTSMOUTH

Preface

The Church is concerned with many things, but its chief task is to do with God. As the body of Christ, we find ourselves called to explore the ways of God among men and women and, in doing so, to announce that the presence here of the God who is Father of Jesus Christ is unqualified good news, or 'gospel'.

This theological task is carried out primarily in conversation with the documents of our faith: the holy scriptures. It is here that we have the earliest records of responses to Jesus and the narratives of his life which are closest to the historical events which give rise to them. That history, of course, was never without interpretation. How could it be? Here was a story that told of God focusing the demands of his coming reign in one man; that spoke of God becoming human; that promised access to God for all who would believe that Jesus was alive again after his cruel death. Anything written of such a story was bound to include an element of interpretation along with 'bare' facts. A 'Gospel', in the technical sense, is just such a presentation of the significance of Jesus.

It is to address this reality that commentaries are written, so that those who have made it their business to study the scriptures at some depth, length, and with some leisure to do so, may share their insights and so inform the reading of other people. Commentaries suggest possible ways of reading, not simply to instruct, but also to invite a broadening of understanding.

The decision of the General Synod of the Church of England to adopt the *Revised Common Lectionary* for its scheme of biblical readings in public worship puts it alongside a large number of other Christian denominations. It also ensures that the range and balance of the biblical material that is covered is more satisfactory than has been the case in recent years, and it removes from its worship the tyranny of the 'theme', which has tended to dominate the interpretation of the biblical passages selected. One feature of the *Revised Common Lectionary* is its use of consecutive reading of the Bible. Such an approach cannot but help in assisting the people of God to become more keenly aware of the riches of holy scripture. If this, the lectionary, is used sensibly in exposition and preaching, it can become a powerful tool in making Christian people more aware of how the Bible might be used in aiding discipleship.

The invitation to edit this commentary and to write a part of it was irresistible. Moreover, it was a particular delight to be able to undertake the task with the help of such colleagues as Georgiana Heskins and Stephen Motyer. The three of us represent different traditions within Anglicanism, but we share a love for the scriptures worked out in their detailed study and a conviction about their status in the piety of Christian people.

We have been supported in our work by the delightful encouragement of Christine Smith of the Canterbury Press, the patience of our families and colleagues and a great sense that what we were doing was a worthwhile project – to encourage the reading of the scriptures themselves.

MARTIN KITCHEN
Southwark
Holy Week 1997

Introduction

On Reading St Luke's Gospel

Many who read the four Gospels probably do so with the assumption that these documents provide us with different perspectives on the life of the historical figure of Jesus of Nazarath. What may not impinge very much on our consciousness is that there are, in fact, different versions of the life of Jesus. It may be possible to use them to construct, with a greater or lesser degree of accuracy, a chronological account of the life of Jesus, but we need to be aware that the purpose of the Gospels is not to furnish the reader with information about a life which lies beyond or behind the written record. What each evangelist wrote was the life as he knew and understood it; and therein lies the challenge and delight of biblical scholarship.

We have St Luke to thank for many of the stories which are part of Christian culture. The parables of the Lost Coin, the Lost Sheep and the Prodigal Son are all stories that Luke has handed down to us. From him we learn of the angels and the shepherds at the birth of Jesus, and of the encounter on the road to Emmaus at the resurrection. It is he who tells of the Ascension, both in the Gospel and in the Acts of the Apostles, and it is he who, in the later volume, makes such a striking narrative of the gift of the Holy Spirit at Pentecost.

It is now commonly accepted among scholars that there exists an important level of interdependence between the first three Gospels. The fact that they can be placed alongside one another in a synopsis, so that the similarities between them can be studied, is what has given them the title 'Synoptic Gospels'. The precise relationship between them, however, is disputed. That St Mark's is the earliest is the most widely agreed conclusion, though even this is contested by some. The two Gospels of Matthew and Luke have much material in common, and an argument rages over whether the two used a common source, or one used the other. This debate becomes even more hotly contested when questions of authenticity and historicity are addressed with reference to individual paragraphs in the narrative.

In the case of Luke, we also need to remember that the Gospel which is traditionally ascribed to him is the first of a two-part work which is completed in the Acts of the Apostles. We have from him, then, an understanding of the Christian movement that takes the whole of its early history very seriously; here was something which had its origins in a Jewish past, which was centred upon the life of Jesus of Nazareth, and which continued in the story of the Christian mission begun by Peter and Paul. One commentator entitled his commentary *The Middle of Time.* He thus brought into focus the sense in which the story of Jesus is the mid-point between the story of the Jewish people of God and their universal counterpart, the people of God which includes the whole of humanity. Luke's broad and universal outlook is featured in the story he tells of Jesus. The good news which Jesus both preaches and embodies is inclusive and all-embracing. Outsiders, whether they are ritually impure, or foreign, or outlawed, are all included in the kingdom of God which Jesus ushers in. Even a dying thief is told, 'Today you will be with me in paradise.'

The tradition that Luke, the companion of St Paul, was the author of the third Gospel and of the Acts of the Apostles goes back at least as far as Irenaeus in 180 CE. The Gospel must have been written after Mark's, since it is dependent upon Mark, and before 130 CE, because Marcion used it. Some scholars narrow this time in various ways, but we cannot be certain of any precise dating. However, we do know that Luke was a gifted story-teller; that he was committed to the life of the continuing Christian community; and that he believed in the universal nature of the Christian Gospel.

In deciding a title for the present volume and the two which follow it, one thing that became clear was that such a title must draw attention to a conviction that the scriptures embody, in some sense, the Word of God to humankind. What God addresses to us is, primarily, his Son, the Word incarnate, and the scriptures, as written documents, bear witness to this primary Word. However, there is also a sense in which the written record itself may also be called 'the Word', and St Luke's Gospel suggests that one of the ways in which this 'Word' might be summed up is as the 'Word of Life'. Here is an understanding of the life of Jesus; here also begins a story of the life of the earliest Christian communities. More importantly, however, this Gospel constitutes the invitation to life which is implicit in the story of Jesus, and which Luke makes his own by the very openness and universalism of his approach to it. This volume, *Word of Life*, will be followed by *Word of Promise* in Year A, when the Gospel readings will be from St Matthew, and *Word of Truth* in Year B, when they will come from St Mark.

Word of Life

The First Sunday of Advent

Jeremiah 33:14–16
Psalm 25:1–10
1 Thessalonians 3:9–13
Luke 21:25–36

L IVING at the dawn of a new millennium, we are familiar with
the spirit of many of our Advent texts. We have become
accustomed to the warning that our generation will be the last and
tend to take this with a pinch of salt, preferring to believe that
nothing much that we can do will make any difference anyway. In
any case, this millennial movement, like others before it, will slip
away into the sand with the non-arrival of the End. If we are not
paralysed by our apparent powerlessness, we may take the different
– equally hazardous – route of over-confidence in our religious
inheritance. The people of God have always appealed to an
unconditional covenant – and Christian people are more prone
than most to complacency. The Advent readings help us to chart a
more exhilarating course as we look again at a bizarre juxtaposition
of themes of penitence and rejoicing in this pre-Christmas season.

Jeremiah understood the upheavals of his time to be God's judgment, and he proclaimed a difficult and unpopular message about
the complacency of religious people and their over-confidence in
the covenant. Ultimately, according to today's reading, Judah will
be saved and God's promises fulfilled in justice and righteousness.
This happy outcome involves a change of heart, however; a life-
change – exile and return – epitomized in a new line of rulers who
trace their ancestry to David. The new name of Jerusalem will be
'The Lord our Righteousness', to show that the city is finally
exemplifying that holiness which is appropriate for her covenant
relationship. Beyond disaster lies a hope rooted in a bond which
God is willing to maintain.

Questions about 'the end' constitute a significant theme in Paul's
letter to the Christians at Thessalonica and, at this early stage in his
mission, he clearly expects 'the coming of the Lord Jesus with all
his saints' very soon. There is an urgency here which we can heed.
It matters for us to be prepared to stand before God at any time,

3

whether at the end of the world or at the end of our lives. What happens to us in the next life depends on the kind of people we have managed to become during this one. When we die we will know the consequences of what we did or did not do when we had the chance. We too need to have our hearts 'strengthen[ed] ... in holiness' before we know ourselves as we are known.

Judgment starts now, and its note is again sounded in the bizarre story of the fig tree in today's Gospel. It brings us to the heart of a penitential theme, with knotty questions of responsibility. (Luke may well be reflecting some of the despondency felt by Christians at their mistreatment in the cause of the Christian mission.) Some guilt is inappropriate, such as when the 'victim' of crime is both exploited and blamed for it. Such shame is corrosive and can never aid the creative living of a life. We rightly tell each other from time to time that we should not always lay the blame either on ourselves or on others; but we neglect at our peril a proper sense of shame for the suffering which our actions *do* cause. How else will we make the strenuous efforts needed to live a better life? The pessimism from which Luke's readers are exhorted to 'look up' is not the end of the story, but hearts need to be strengthened for holiness; we need to recognize open-eyed both the blame and the glory, the failure and recovery, as our redemption draws near.

* * *

The Second Sunday of Advent

Baruch 5:1–9 *or* Malachi 3:1–4
Canticle: Benedictus
Philippians 1:3–11
Luke 3:1–6

TODAY'S uncomfortable picture is of road-building in desert places – the irreversible changing of a familiar landscape in preparation for God's coming. The process takes years, and inhospitable conditions in the environment or the weather cause delays and frustration. New roads carve through the landscape, some-

4

times without respect for its undulations, its woodlands or its wildlife. The levelled place has drainage problems which the natural landscape never knew. A well-used road needs constantly re-working and re-building. The 'motorway maintenance' teams take over from the construction company and the cones move eternally from one stretch of road to the next.

Just as road-making is uncomfortable and road use reveals design faults, so travel reveals our imperfections. A journey together is the surest test of friendship. The Christian pilgrimage takes us, by way of the thirsty desert, to a level place where repentance is required, where all flesh shall see the salvation of God – this is identified here with 'all the region around Jordan'. In Luke 3 we move from faithful Judaism, exemplified by Anna and Simeon in the Temple, to a world stage and the public arena.

Whereas in the past the river of healing was believed to flow only from the Temple in Jerusalem – a known, safe and religious place – now John is preaching a baptism of repentance in a dangerous and apparently barren place. This is in stark contrast to the tangle and confusion which underlies our so-called rich and fulfilling lives. It is a reminder that the plethora of opportunities which surround us need to be negotiated with some care. God is sometimes only heard in profound aloneness, in what has been called 'sounding silence'. Can silence be for us a resource from which we speak and live the gospel?

The Lord comes like a refiner's fire – and like fuller's soap – to purify us. Purity may not be one of our favourite words. It sometimes suggests a lack of courage, a lack of risk and of initiative. It is associated with innocence and untaintedness, inexperience and virginity, and is not greatly admired. We prefer maturity: the ability to hold to a course with integrity and without distraction, to speak the truth whatever that may cost, to live faithfully and comfortably in our own skins, to be single-minded and yet unshockable by the unfamiliar. John's baptism, humiliating as it is for those who have to bow to it, is the only way to strip down to the essentials. They say the tasks of old age are mostly about divesting ourselves of powers and possessions, and perhaps that is not so far from purification after all.

5

For Baruch there is the reminder that this dispossession, this level-ling, is undertaken by God. Malachi presumes that it will be uncomfortable. Why do we associate God's coming with an easier life? What a mistake! The Canticle – the Benedictus – promises compassion and peace, to be sure, but notice the past tense. The picture of dawn breaking so mercifully can perhaps only be painted with hindsight. Today we can only see the familiar being carved up, uncomfortably, in preparation for God's coming.

★　★　★

The Third Sunday of Advent

Zephaniah 3:14–20
Canticle: Isaiah 12:2–6
Philippians 4:4-7
Luke 3:7–18

HOMECOMING is an evocative metaphor for returning to where we belong, putting down roots in the hope of some conti-nuity. Zephaniah appealed for a remnant to repent and seek their home in the Lord, so that the people of Israel might be renewed. The royal line is to be restored. So too in the Lucan passage: God is able to raise a future generation – name-bearers of faith – from lifeless stones. The message of hope is that God is near. The dawning of a day of justice, truth and equality rests on the promise of God's peace. It is the peace which is recounted in the Canticle from Isaiah, which holds a proclamation against despair and another image of settled homeliness: women and children drawing water from the village well.

Those whom Luke describes as 'filled with expectation', ques-tioning whether John was the Messiah, are an intriguing bunch exemplified by tax collectors and soldiers. In the Gospels, tax collectors are a despised group – those who profit from their own people on behalf of the occupying force. Soldiers are also entrusted with this honour, due to the ruling system. Both occupations were more open than most to bribery and extortion. John asks for a change in behaviour. This is a preamble; there is a sense in which the kingdom of God presupposes the equality of human beings and our consequent responsibility to make ourselves ready in terms, already known to us, of fairness and honesty. There is a comparison to be made between what John is asking – a change in behaviour based on known principles – and the change that is coming after which goes profoundly inward. The one who baptizes with unquenchable fire will probe at deeper levels of consciousness and take us into realms beyond control and containment. The wells of salvation (Isaiah 12:3) may not, after all, be domesticated.

For Luke, Jesus is *par excellence* the one who lives by what he proclaims. He too will be baptized by John. He too will be tempted by the devil's bribery, before he can truly return home to Nazareth. And even then it will not be the comfortable homecoming which we associate with the settled life.

* * *

The Fourth Sunday of Advent

Micah 5:2–5a
Magnificat *or* Psalm 80:1–7
Hebrews 10:5–10
Luke 1:39–45 (*or* 39–55)

WHEREAS in the early Sundays of Advent the images which predominate are tough and uncomfortable, now, on the threshold of Christmas, it is images of restoration which take precedence over those of judgment. There is the language of peace and security in Micah; of the Shepherd of Israel in Psalm 80 (a psalm probably from the nomadic, northern tribes); and, in the Magnificat, of the poor and hungry being fed. The words of Mary are the foretaste of Luke's 'theology of the poor': his vision of the Christian community as one where priority is accorded to the utterly destitute, those who have to survive on the breadline.

It sounds good. We happily affirm the vision of the 'lift[ing] up [of] the lowly' and of the 'hungry ... filled with good things', forgetting, perhaps, that the tax collectors and soldiers, those with a steady income, are required to make the dream a reality. Mary's Magnificat gives her, in Luke's Gospel, the role of the ideal disciple – she who hears the word and acts on it for the salvation of the poor and downtrodden. For Luke, Jesus' physical family has to meet the criteria of discipleship. The Old Testament background to Mary's song suggests that her blessing is not a purely private one. Just as Hannah in 1 Samuel 1–3 is the prophetic heroine of her people, so Luke esteems Mary as the first Christian disciple. She has spoken out for the poor and destitute and in her obedience shows herself to be the true disciple of Jesus, whose own life was also lived in radical obedience to God.

The theme of obedience is again present in the reading from Hebrews 10. Here the author puts words of Psalm 40 on the lips of Jesus, identifying Jesus' life and death as an obedient self-offering which abrogates the whole sacrificial system. Scripture witnesses to Jesus, who may therefore be said to speak through it. The indication that obedience will entail suffering allows the shadow of the cross to fall across the proclamation of the nativity.

Even before his birth, John the Baptist has begun to act as a prophet in hailing Jesus as the Messiah. Elizabeth's Canticle in praise of Mary, like the Magnificat which follows it, is a mosaic of Old Testament allusion. We may never be sure whether the songs were actually sung by Christian groups known to the evangelist, but it is clearly his intention that we make them our own. In the shorter Canticle, Elizabeth praises Mary the mother, the first disciple. Mary then transfers the praise to God. The destinies of the unborn John the Baptist and the unborn Jesus are both confirmed as divinely upheld. The 'Shepherd of Israel' will 'feed his flock in the strength of the Lord' and we look forward to the moment when very lowly shepherds will also hear the announcement of 'Glory to God ... and peace on earth'.

*   *   *

Christmas Day

First set of readings
Isaiah 9:2–7
Psalm 96
Titus 2:11–14
Luke 2:1–14 (*or* 1–20)

THE first set of readings for Christmas Day stresses the theme that God reveals his salvation to outsiders; sometimes they are foreigners, and sometimes they are people who are ordinarily overlooked, excluded or assailed by difficulties. Like the other readings, this set includes a passage from Isaiah as the Old Testament text and one of the 'royal psalms' as the Canticle. The New Testament authors believed that the divine promises to David had been fulfilled in Jesus, so passages from Isaiah or the Psalter which had come to have a messianic interpretation within Judaism were taken to refer to him, and Jesus was understood to preside over the final age of a renewed creation. The passage from Isaiah 9 is a good example of the way in which ancient prophecy was interpreted and re-interpreted to meet each new situation. Galilee, the northern region of Palestine, was known as a place of mixed race – the land of the Gentiles. In the New Testament it functions as a symbol for the breadth of Jesus' inclusive vision grounded in an actual ministry in the real world. This passage may originally have celebrated the accession of a Judean king, but in its present context it describes the promised Messiah as the ideal 'once and future' ruler of his people.

The letter to Titus seems to be a collection of instructions written late in the New Testament period to urban Christians assailed by false teaching of an extreme and secret kind. The context is specific, but the theology upon which the author's guidance rests is pure 'good news'. The life-style of individuals and communities is grounded in God's love. This is no secret; Jesus Christ communicates the transcendent God and we are all to anticipate Christ's 'appearing' – an expression which encompasses both his first coming 'in the flesh' and his return at the End. These Christians are to live, unashamed, in that light.

Luke's Gospel, like the letter to Titus, narrates a universal and public setting for a universal Saviour: the *fiat* of an earthly Caesar can be used in the will of God. Luke stresses the intrinsic connection between the birth of the Messiah and what has preceded in Israel. Where John the Baptist's birth was greeted by prophecy, this scene goes further: there is an angelic proclamation of the significance of the new-born child. The manger and shepherds underline the incongruous circumstances: God reveals his salvation to a group of despised 'outsiders' – and this theme will be pursued throughout Jesus' ministry.

*   *   *

Christmas Day

Second set of readings
Isaiah 62:6–12
Psalm 97
Titus 3:4–7
Luke 2:1–7 (*or* 1–20)

THE passages from Isaiah set for the Christmas season reflect different points in Israel's history, for which prophetic interpretation was called. Many themes of the earliest period of Isaiah of Jerusalem (eighth century BCE) are then extended and reinterpreted in the light of subsequent experience in the sixth century BCE. The result is an extraordinarily richly layered text which became a favourite source of language and meaning for New Testament authors exploring the mystery of Jesus' identity. This passage from Isaiah 62 is about the restoration of Jerusalem after the exiles' return from Babylon. The prophetic sentinels sound out from the ruined walls claiming universal renown for the city. The past history of foreign invaders plundering the harvest contrasts with a new and settled life-style.

This message of hope fulfilled is continued in the Psalm. The language is strikingly similar to the passage from Isaiah. It celebrates the kingship of God, the dawn of a new age, the worship and praise of the Creator who rules with justice, a universal setting for a universal Saviour.

10

The letter to Titus reminds us that all loving action has its source in God's grace. Our lives are to be lived in anticipation of Christ's 'appearing' – an expression which encompasses both his first coming 'in the flesh' and his return as judge at the End. He is the communication of the transcendent God within the created order and his servants should not be ashamed of the chains they may have to wear as subversives in an alien empire. In this way the author both makes Christian teaching public (in contrast to the esoteric claims of the false teachers he opposes) and also gives value to his readers' sense of being in the world but not of it.

Luke similarly describes a public setting for Jesus' birth. He stresses continuity with the past: the fulfilment of prophecy and of the hopes of humble, faithful people. The manger and the shepherds underline the incongruous circumstances; the angels remind us that this is no ordinary baby. Finally, Mary embodies a smooth continuity between Israel and the Christian movement. She responds obediently to God's word as a faithful Jew and appears in Jesus' ministry as a faithful disciple. Meanwhile she 'treasured all these words and pondered them in her heart'. Luke wants to encourage all of us along the same Christian way in a spirit of prayerfulness and joy.

* * *

Christmas Day

Third set of readings
Isaiah 52:7–10
Psalm 98
Hebrews 1:1–4 (*or* 1–12)
John 1:1–14

THE third set of readings for Christmas Day stresses continuity with the past, with Jesus as the fulfilment of all the expectations of Israel, and the fact that this birth embodies a great mystery. The passage from Isaiah 52 reflects the period of exile in Babylon and the message of hope proclaimed by sentinels from the ruined walls of Jerusalem. It captures the breadth of vision discovered in

11

captivity. Not only were the exiles able to sing the Lord's song in a strange land, but ultimately their God – the God of Israel – would be acknowledged as Creator of all the earth and Saviour of the nations.

At the very outset of the letter to the Hebrews, we find that the author understands the whole revelation of God throughout history to be focused on Jesus. Judaism and Christianity have not yet gone their separate ways and for this author it is faithfulness to God which is the issue, whatever the route. The inspiration of the past is affirmed. The word spoken through the Son is the fulfilment of a diverse divine address spoken through the prophets. Two themes are entwined in these few verses: continuity with the past and the supreme revelation in Christ. The author begins with an appeal to what was already known and accepted by his audience. God's active involvement with creation has been constant from the very beginning; Jesus, the new Wisdom, personifies that involvement. He alone is God's last word. For this author it was the life and work of Jesus of Nazareth, not a set of writings alone, which was the norm by which all inherited religious traditions were to be judged.

The prologue to John's Gospel, like the letter to the Hebrews, describes Jesus in language previously applied by Judaism to Wisdom and the Word. Its hymn-like poetry which extols his role in creation and redemption is entirely distinctive among the Gospels but, like the nativity stories in Matthew and Luke, it seeks to establish God's purpose in the birth of Jesus. His human origins are acknowledged and his humanity is witnessed, but the Gospel of John will set out to prove that Jesus is also the final revealer of God.

* * *

The First Sunday of Christmas

1 Samuel 2:18–20
Psalm 148
Colossians 3:12–17
Luke 2:41–52

CHRISTMAS continues with an exploration of seasonal themes. 'Who is this child?' and 'What is his destiny?' are questions which Luke's Gospel has already attempted to answer on the lips of angels and shepherds. Today we pick up the same questions, but the location has shifted from Bethlehem to the Temple in Jerusalem and the answers are given not by interested spectators but by the child Jesus himself. The other readings may be seen to reinforce his answers.

The Old Testament parallel gives us the picture of the parents of Samuel going up once a year to worship at the sanctuary of Shiloh. Similarly, Joseph and Mary are upright Jews who observed the Law. Tradition has it that Samuel began his prophetic career at the age of twelve with a call from God, as described in 1 Samuel 3. Luke's telling of the story of Jesus is deeply coloured by these Old Testament passages. In his treatment of Mary he surely has in mind Samuel's mother Hannah (her name means 'grace' or 'favour'), and the Magnificat resonates with Hannah's song in 1 Samuel 2:1–10. This little cameo of maternal devotion and sacrifice is the context out of which Samuel's life as God's prophet will begin. Psalm 148, a great paean of praise for God's universal glory, extends the notion of God's election of individuals to that of a chosen community 'who are close to him'.

The reading from Colossians echoes the way in which the Old Testament was able to move between the themes of chosen individuals and elect people. Here it is the significance of Jesus for the believing Church, his Body, which is being explored. As the Gospel reading establishes the continuity of the Christian movement with Israel, so the Colossian letter teases out its implications: Christ, the chosen one of God – the true Israel – has been raised to glory. Those 'in Christ' are therefore the new 'people of God', called into one body. Differences notwithstanding, the Colossian

Christians are to clothe themselves with love and manifest the same wisdom and worship as Jesus, the Son of God, showed in his lifetime.

The story told in today's Gospel, unique in the New Testament, is given in preparation for the adult ministry of Jesus which Luke begins to describe in the next chapter. The young Jesus listens and asks questions of the teachers of Israel, stressing his piety and his interest in the Law. More importantly, he refers to God as his Father and so delineates the nature of his life work as the obedient 'Son of God'. The scene is set in Jerusalem, the city of destiny for Jesus, and in the Temple, which in Luke and the Acts of the Apostles is pre-eminently the place where Christianity emerges. Of the prophet Samuel, too, it was written that 'he grew up in the presence of the Lord' (1 Samuel 1:21); Luke's echo of this in verse 52 constitutes Jesus' transition to his ministry at the age of thirty. The continuity of the Christian movement with Israel is thereby established, but even Mary, representative of the ideals of discipleship, would not fully recognize Jesus as 'Son of God' until after his resurrection.

* * *

The Second Sunday of Christmas

Jeremiah 31:7–14 *and* Psalm 147:17–20 *or* Ecclesiasticus 24:1–12 *and* Wisdom of Solomon 10:15–21
Ephesians 1:3–14
John 1:1–9 *or* 1–18

THE language of homecoming, abundant in readings for Advent, reappears as fulfilled in the incarnation. The Second Sunday of Christmas gives us an opportunity to think some more about where Jesus' 'home' is. We re-visit the first chapter of John's Gospel to find that this evangelist avoids the Bethlehem birth stories of Matthew and Luke. Perhaps he did not know them or, more likely, he was not satisfied with them as adequate explanations of Jesus' divine origins. He contrasts an ultimate, heavenly, home with outward appearances. Jesus is the son of Joseph from

14

Nazareth and his humanity is assumed, but he is also Son of God – in complete communion with the Eternal One (v. 18). Despite their otherworldiness, Jesus' human origins are not a matter to be overcome. They remain with him and are underlined in eyewitness accounts (vv. 14, 15). It is to his own place that he comes, but his own people will not accept him. The shadow of rejection hangs over this homecoming, but as the revealer and Word of God his origin and ultimate calling lie elsewhere. We are faced with the same choice as the original witnesses: to receive him or to refuse him.

If we receive him, Jesus' calling as the beloved Son of God can be ours as well because we are Christians. The letter to the Ephesians understands the Church as the truly elected Israel. As Christ's body it is called to participate in the mission of the covenant people, a mission of service and proclamation to the world. It also inherits the accomplishments of Christ's death – notably freedom and forgiveness won by sacrifice. Like Christ, the head of the body, all Christians are sealed with the Spirit and share his ultimate destiny in God. Our homecoming will be to know ourselves as God's own people, to the praise of his glory. What God has planned since before creation has now come to be.

The Old Testament readings and Canticles set for this Sunday maintain the language of homecoming. In the passage from Jeremiah the return from exile in Babylon is described as transcending the exodus of old from Egypt. It will not be fraught with the same hazards as the children of Israel encountered in the desert. The language of 'redemption' (buying back the freedom of slaves) is reminiscent of another prophet of the exilic period – the author(s) of Isaiah 40–55, known as Second Isaiah. The New Testament authors – among them the author of Ephesians – discovered in this imagery, and particularly in these prophecies, a rich language with which to describe the significance of Jesus. Praises will be raised to God for deliverance, and bountiful produce in a settled homeland will mark the new age of well-being. It is a vision of a better world to which the redeemed in Christ are also asked to respond.

Another image seized upon by early Christians in their struggle to find adequate language for Jesus is that of Wisdom. We are offered an alternative Old Testament reading from Ecclesiasticus in which personified Wisdom, the agent of salvation, searches for a resting place. She is equated with the creative word of God and with Torah. Paul calls Christ the wisdom of God (in 1 Corinthians 1:24) and the mini-creation story at the beginning of the Gospel passage (John 1:1–3) consciously evokes another wisdom passage from Proverbs 8. Wisdom has enjoyed something of a revival in recent years as contemporary theology looks for ways of countering the patriarchal images of God with some feminine alternatives. It remains a matter of conjecture as to how far these passages have been influenced by beliefs about the goddess Wisdom of Egyptian and Mesopotamian religion, but it is unlikely that pre-Christian Judaism understood her as a divine being independent of the God of Israel. In our passages, therefore, she affirms that the divine calling and covenant with creation has been preserved from the very beginning. The God whom we worship is to be found 'at home' in the world.

* * *

The Epiphany

Isaiah 60:1–6
Psalm 72:1–9 *or* 1–15
Ephesians 3:1–12
Matthew 2:1–12

To travel purposefully requires some sense of direction. We find the way by asking the right questions of the right people. The journey of the season of Epiphany, which begins today with the visit of the mysterious 'wise men' to the infant Jesus, is all about mission. It is our calling as Christians to make Christ 'manifest'. Having celebrated the presence of God incarnate in the creation, we turn outwards from the manger and the crib to ask questions of ourselves and others about the direction in which to travel if we are to be faithful to God's mission in the world.

In the Old Testament reading, the exiles are journeying to rebuild Jerusalem. They have asked difficult questions in Babylon and

16

have lamented their absence from the land of promise. But their discoveries represent a great step forward in religious understanding: not only the exiles of Judah but the riches of Arabia are to be brought by camel caravan in proclamation of the praise of the God of Israel. The Creator God is not a tribal deity, but has given his people a universal mission.

Psalm 72 reinforces this extraordinary insight. It is a prayer for guidance for the king, perhaps to be used in commemoration of his crowning as God's representative, but again his responsibilities extend well beyond his own borders. The promise is that the kings of Tarshish and of the isles shall render him tribute, and gold of Sheba shall be given to him. The health, fertility and success of all the nations are bound up with the messianic king of Israel.

Many of the questions about the Gentile mission in New Testament times can only be guessed from passages such as the one set for our New Testament reading today. Clearly, Paul suffered during his lifetime for the conviction that God had called the Gentiles to be part of the redeemed community; but because, in the end, it was this point of view which won the day we hear less from the other side. The mystery, or secret, is that Gentiles are to form an integral part of the new Israel. God's answer, his wisdom in the plan of redemption, maps the direction for the community of faith.

The visitors from the East received the proclamation of Jesus' birth by a star; the natural world gives them the beginning of an answer to their questions, but they soon come to realize that the end of the journey is not where they had anticipated. The full revelation of the messiah cannot be gleaned from nature: it is a secret, so Matthew maintains, found buried in the scriptures. The religious leaders, it seems, know the prophecies but are not asking the questions. Herod takes the questions and answers seriously but is also threatened by the messiah, and so rejects him. Only the wise men make the journey. So affected are they by their discovery of the Christ child that they worship and are given the direction for their return – a route that presents them with new challenges in their own place.

The Baptism of Christ

Isaiah 43:1–7
Psalm 29
Acts 8:14–17
Luke 3:15–17, 21–22

THE symbols of water and fire, offered to us today, give us further opportunity to explore the theme of the season: the mission of the Church in its witness to Christ's coming among us. Both may be seen as powerful signs that the creative life of the Spirit takes root in some surprising places. God 'broods' over all parts of our experience and is to be found in the most baffling and the most potentially destructive places. We are to be warned and encouraged by God's mysterious sovereignty within the disorder of our world.

For the exiles in Babylon, Israel is God's unique possession, sometimes described as 'servant' or as 'son'. Both water and fire are perceived as dangerous: not to be avoided, but to be encountered without either being swept away or burned alive. God, the prophet maintains, protects the people through all their journeyings and adventures as their Creator and Redeemer. In the Old Testament – as in all religious traditions – the natural elements have positive and negative connotations. Water is the source of life, and it is the chaos out of which creation is fashioned and ordered. The Psalm remind us that 'the Lord is enthroned over the flood'. Similarly, 'the voice of the Lord strikes with flashes of lighting'; fire gives heat and light, it refines and purges. As a symbol of judgment it is not to be under-estimated. It is powerful for both good and ill.

The message of Acts, from which the New Testament reading is taken, finds expression in an exploration of the Church as a community called to bear witness to Jesus. Right at the beginning, the coming of the Holy Spirit in tongues of flame and rushing wind is interpreted as power for this task. Pentecost is seen as the fulfilment of prophecy with signs of the last days now given to 'all flesh'. Thereafter the Spirit is continually active in the Church and, as in this passage, is given to people at the point of water baptism or shortly afterwards. The presence of the Spirit is a sign that God is at work.

As we have seen in relation to Acts, the Spirit occupies an integral place in the theology of Luke. For this evangelist the empowering of Jesus occurs shortly after his baptism in the Jordan, while he is praying, and marks him out as the unique 'son' of God, the true and obedient Israel. As at creation, the Spirit broods over the waters of chaos, in order to bring life out of them. The coming of the Holy Spirit upon Jesus is presented as the divine response to his obedience and openness to God. It is a powerful personal experience, but there is nothing private about it. As at Pentecost, it results in a new fire of energetic service and preaching, and in the formation of a praying community.

* * *

The Second Sunday of Epiphany

Isaiah 62:1–5
Psalm 36:5–10
1 Corinthians 12:1–11
John 2:1–11

WE know that children need love and security if they are to produce their best, and that if others believe in them they are more likely to believe in themselves. As adults we too need affirmation and affection; the profound and mutual understanding sometimes celebrated in marriage. A similarly reciprocal revelation is being proclaimed in today's readings – it is the symbol of a wedding feast by which we are encouraged to explore the 'mission' theme in this Epiphany season.

In the reading from Isaiah it is Zion who is revealed as God's beloved. As the return from exile is anticipated, so it is understood as a reconciliation between the Lord and his people: a nation brought home to their own land with a new name. As they know themselves to be the object of delight, so their joy and beauty will be plain for all to see. After all, all the world loves a lover. The

19

Psalm praises the abundant generosity of God as Lover – 'you [who] give them drink from the river of your delights'. The theme of light, given and received, underlines that the initiative lies with God but that the effects are uncontainable and far-reaching.

Just as the returning exiles understood themselves called to be a light to the nations, so too the 'new' Israel has a similar mission. God's people are always called to an adult relationship of mutual delight, for the sake of the whole world. But just as we have a tendency to sentimentalize love and marriage, so we do in our dealings with the Lord. Paul, writing to the Corinthians, points to the activity of the Holy Spirit as the sign of God's revelation, but it is not ecstasy which proves it. The test for the Body of Christ is whether the diverse gifts contribute to the common good; only in this way will they manifest God's presence. Christians constitute one body for that purpose.

Revelation is a two-way process. John's Gospel, in exploring Jesus' task to reveal the Father, points also to the Church's task to go beyond known religious categories in the same abundant generosity of self-giving love. The wine, constantly poured out for the life and delight of God's creatures, is for ever new and will always surprise us. We too are called to delight and surprise our Creator. The best wine, which will nourish the mission in which all are called to share, is yet to be.

*　　*　　*

The Third Sunday of Epiphany

Nehemiah 8:1–3, 5–6, 8–10
Psalm 19
1 Corinthians 12:12–31a
Luke 4:14–21

THE turning of the year has brought us, with Jesus, back home to Nazareth for the discovery of mission as the proclaiming of 'good news' to the poor and imprisoned. Mid-winter celebrations, in the northern hemisphere at least, are now over. The commu-

20

nity, armed with new year resolution, has gathered again to redefine its *raison d'être* and renew its promises.

In popular belief the Feast of Tabernacles, the ancient New Year's Day, was a foretaste of the great Day of the Lord, a final climax of history when God would fulfil the covenant promise. The reading from Nehemiah describes the restoration of the Temple and the covenant after the people's return from exile. They are to gather and to read from the Law of God and to interpret it for their own times. The Canticle underlines that God's mission, as revealed both in the wonders of nature and in scripture, will revive, enlighten and rejoice them.

For Paul, too, the gathered community, and the way it organizes itself for mission, is a prime concern. God's gifts are revealed in the body of Christ, and most particularly in its weaker members. Baptism defines this new social reality, cutting across all the conventional distinctions of race and gender. For Paul, the ethical life is the work of God, the consequence, not the condition, of membership of the Body. Paul expects the Day of the Lord imminently, and this lends urgency to his strategy for mission and to his appeal to the Corinthian Christians to exercise their gifts of prophecy, healing and teaching.

Jesus' homecoming to the Nazareth synagogue reveals the nature of his ministry. He reads the great prophecy in one of the last chapters of the book of Isaiah. It announces that God's appointed one will come with the power of God's Spirit to bring good news to the poor, release to captives and sight to the blind ... but he interrupts the reading before it goes on to announce the 'day of vengeance'. It is as if he wants to underline the last part of the quotation: 'to proclaim the year of the Lord's favour' – a new year of Jubilee, the true and final one, in which slaves are liberated and all debts are cancelled. His life and ministry will be characterized by all that is most gracious and positive. The community which gathers in his name, to make its own new year pledges, will be similarly gifted by the Spirit of God for a mission which brings hope and liberation to the most oppressed. Most of all it is a community in which all can make a new start, recognizing their indebtedness.

21

The Fourth Sunday of Epiphany

Ezekiel 43:27–44:4
Psalm 48
1 Corinthians 13:1–13
Luke 2:22–40

L OVE is always costly. It involves giving away a part of who we are, opening ourselves to the possibility of loss, even of rejection. But still we say: 'Better to have loved and lost, than never to have loved at all.' If we choose to affirm life we may also risk love – though we will learn painfully to count the cost and to be parted by death from those we love. Today's readings enable us to explore what is revealed of God in seeing the mission of Jesus – and of the people of God – as involving suffering. The Epiphany season has given us less cryptic pictures: a star, gold and frankincense, a wedding feast with wine. But Simeon's soul-piercing sword, like the magi's myrrh, offers an image which points to more sombre events.

The Old Testament reading establishes the Temple of Ezekiel's vision as the holy place to which God returns to be with his people. Psalm 48 similarly praises God's glory on the mountain, in the city and 'in the midst of your temple'. The setting of the Temple on the 'hill of the Lord' recalls us to very ancient holy places of revelation. For the New Testament authors the days of the Temple were numbered, and after 70 CE its cult was replaced in Christian imagination with alternative allusions. Whether it was an image originally used of Jesus and subsequently transferred to the church, or vice versa, the Christian community soon saw itself as the new Temple, and it is this tradition which we find in Paul's first letter to the Corinthians: 'Surely you know that you are God's temple and that God's Spirit lives in you!' (1 Corinthians 3:16). Following on immediately from his description of the baptized community as the Body of Christ, the hymn to love set for today is a reminder that the dwelling place of the Holy Spirit is revealed less in outward displays than in costly endurance: 'Love ... bears all things, believes all things, hopes all things.' The way of love is also the way of suffering.

In Luke's Gospel the Temple is again strikingly prominent. Here it represents the faithful Judaism of Anna and Simeon. But elsewhere in the two volumes of Luke and Acts a less favourable attitude is expressed: 'The Most High does not live in dwellings made by human hands' (Acts 7:48). Like the prince of Ezekiel 44, it is to the Temple that Jesus comes, but whereas the prince enters for a ceremonial meal, Jesus' final symbolic action there propels him to his death. Simeon's prophecy over the young child recognizes the universal salvation which he represents, but he knows, too, that Love can only invite a response – never force it. The invitation to share in his mission will be welcomed and accepted by some – contradicted and rejected by others.

*   *   *

The Presentation of Christ

Malachi 3:1–5
Psalm 24:1–10 *or* 7–10
Hebrews 2:14–18
Luke 2:22–40

WITH this festival we reach the climax of the Christmas cycle and must take a new direction. The Law, the prophetic Spirit and the Temple cult come together to acclaim the greatness of Jesus and to set the scene for the 'consolation' of God's people. The readings reverberate with a gospel mission for the poor and some mysterious bitter-sweet pointers to obedient suffering. Together they are marked by a deep realism and a refusal to oversimplify the complexities of human failure, while at the same time holding confidently to God's promises. We may, perhaps, see their message of hope as a summary of all that this season has celebrated.

The prophecies of Malachi come to us from the period some time after the return from exile. The rebuilding of the Temple is already complete, but the people's heart is no longer in their worship. A new purging of Israel must be undergone before the Lord can fulfil the promise of the nation's glory. The experience of exile has deepened their understanding of God's involvement in their affairs and in this vivid passage the prophet announces the prophetic messenger to prepare the way for the coming of the Lord. The Lord's purpose, first of all, is to refine the religious institutions, purifying the priests until they present 'right offerings'; and then his judgment will fall upon sorcerers, adulterers, false witnesses and those who oppress the poor and defenceless.

'Who is this King of glory?' The question in Psalm 24 echoes the theme of the Epiphany season, and probably reflects an ancient processional liturgy in which the choir requests admission for the Ark of the Covenant. It reinforces the remainder of Christianity's debt to the expectations of ancient Judaism, just as Anna and Simeon, in their welcome of Jesus, point to his replacing of the Temple.

For the author of Hebrews, the Temple has not been replaced either by Jesus or by the Church (as elsewhere in the New Testament). Instead it has been entirely relocated – in heaven. In an innovative use of this image, inspired by Psalm 110, the reading from Hebrews draws on the role of the high priest in the Jewish cult and understands the life, death and exaltation of Jesus primarily in these terms. His solidarity with frail humanity is stressed; but as the exalted and obedient son he is no longer subject to these limitations. He actively guides his followers, encouraging them to make heaven their goal too. This is a Christian community oppressed by earthly constraints but exhorted not to lose heart in God's promises.

The same message of hope and comfort greets Jesus' parents in the Jerusalem Temple. Simeon looks forward to the 'consolation of Israel', echoing the words 'comfort my people' of Isaiah 40. There is similar resonance in his two prophetic oracles: the first proclaiming Jesus, the true Israel, as a light to the Gentiles; the second turning to his destiny as the one who will be rejected by many. Together they hold out an intriguing and exhilarating future. The great hopes of the past are even now being fulfilled by a God who identifies entirely with the circumstances and sufferings of people. We are all called to a confident and sanguine expectation which sets its horizon beyond present limitations or the probability of future pain.

24

The Fifth Sunday before Lent

Isaiah 6:1–8 *or* Isaiah 6:1–13
Psalm 138
1 Corinthians 15:1–11
Luke 5:1–11

EVERY so often our cars need servicing, so we take them to the garage. Many of us find that the same is true of our souls, so we go on retreat. The principle can also be applied to the liturgical year; our worship needs periods at which we take a breather in order to think. So today, after celebrating the Christmas season, ending in the Epiphany and the Presentation, we pause for a few weeks before Lent and have the chance to reflect upon the nature of faith.

We begin in the Temple at Jerusalem, and with Isaiah's vision of the majesty of God. The political situation at the time was critical: the northern kingdom of Israel had been annexed by the Assyrians in 721 BCE, and the southern kingdom, Judah, lived in some fear of what might happen to it. In this context, the prophet Isaiah was called to remind the inhabitants of Judah that their primary responsibility to God involved care for the poor; that the vision of God has a moral implication.

In 1 Corinthians, Paul is both reminding his readers of the basis of their faith in the risen Jesus and asserting his authority as an apostle. For Paul, this meant that the risen Lord had appeared to him personally with a commission to preach.

It is in the context of these two vocations, of the prophet and of the apostle, that we read in the Gospel of the calling of Simon Peter, James and John. The story of the miraculous catch of fish is told in John's Gospel as part of one of the accounts of the resurrection. This may serve to remind us that all the Gospels were written after that event, and are designed to deepen faith in the risen Christ. Simon Peter's response to Jesus is similar to that of Isaiah: he becomes aware of his inadequacy. God's call, however, is not dependent upon a sense of our present capacity to achieve what is required of us; it is rather focused upon what may yet happen if we follow Jesus into the unknown future.

25

Some sense of the majesty of God is a good starting point for reflection upon the nature of our discipleship. Not everybody is granted the ecstatic experience of Isaiah (and some of us may be grateful for that – who could live at such a pitch of enthusiasm and zeal?). But all of us are called to a conviction that Jesus is alive again after his crucifixion, and we have a lifetime to explore both what that means, and how we live out its implications.

For Peter, according to Luke, it was a remarkable catch of fish that persuaded him to start out with Jesus. The life of discipleship begins in the transformation of the everyday. Where it leads is only revealed as we start to accompany Jesus on the road – and there is no knowing where it may take us.

*　　*　　*

The Fourth Sunday before Lent

Jeremiah 17:5–10
Psalm 1
1 Corinthians 15:12–20
Luke 6:17–26

ALL today's readings have something to do with alternatives. For Jeremiah, the choice is between 'those who trust in mere mortals' and 'those who trust in the Lord'; St Paul is concerned to point out the alternative to faith in Christ; and the Gospel contrasts the life which is blessed with the life which is wretched.

Jeremiah was active in Jerusalem at the time of the city's conquest in 587 BCE, and he was taken to Egypt with some of those who were not carried off captive to Babylon. He therefore lived within the tumult of massive upheaval, and part of his message was to insist that what was happening to God's chosen city was the working out of God's judgment. Here he curses those 'whose hearts turn away from the Lord'. The image of a shrub in the desert is one of desolation: it does not know what is happening in the world around. The contrast he draws with the 'tree planted by the water' is therefore one not only of refreshment, life and

26

vigour, but of connection; its roots stretch into the stream and its life is safe, because of its compatibility with what gives it life. The image in Psalm 1 therefore invites a similar interpretation; those who 'do not follow the path of the wicked' do not consort with sinners and scoffers, but live in fruitful relationship with others.

St Paul draws alternatives between a resurrection faith and a life which is without hope if Christ is not raised to life again. The Beatitudes in Luke bear comparison with those in Matthew (5:1–12), and may originate from the same source. Matthew's are longer and more 'spiritual'. Luke's, on the other hand, are more structured, and are balanced by corresponding 'woes'; their emphasis is on material blessing. Matthew tells of Jesus avoiding the crowds and going up a mountain, where he calls his disciples to him and talks to them alone. Luke, on the other hand, says that the disciples of Jesus are a large crowd, and that Jesus addressed them 'on the level place'. He speaks of the values of the reign of God, in which the poor, the hungry, the weeping and the persecuted are blessed; whereas in terms of this world, the rich, the full, the laughing and the well-regarded are all-popular.

However, their problem is that, on their own admission, this is all there is. Once the applause has come and gone, there is nothing left. Only the values of a deeper life, of reflection upon its meaning, only a concern for the reign of God can guarantee blessedness.

What is that blessedness? It is an awareness of the significance of the ways of God, of the kind of behaviour which is of value to God and our neighbours, and of a sense of satisfaction in life which is not dependent upon passing fashion or fleeting acclaim. The alternatives are between curse and blessing; between self-absorption and openness to God; between faith and death.

★   ★   ★

The Third Sunday before Lent

Genesis 45:3–11, 15
Psalm 37:1–11, 39–40
1 Corinthians 15:35–38, 42–50
Luke 6:27–38

'HELL is other people', according to Jean-Paul Sartre – and there are grounds for believing that. Joseph's brothers were particularly cruel, even if they were provoked by his behaviour as his father's favourite (cf. Genesis 37). His forgiveness of them extends to seeing that God was able to bring good out of evil. Such perception is not always possible, and the psalmist's reminder that 'the wicked' and 'wrongdoers' will soon 'fade like the grass, and wither like the green herb' was clearly written long before the twentieth century saw his fellow Jews herded into gas chambers, and their bodies dispersed as ashes into airborne graves.

The argument of 1 Corinthians is generally taken to be St Paul's refutation of those who refuse to believe in the resurrection of the body. The suggestion is that, though Greeks were well familiar with the doctrine of the immortality of the soul, they could not accept the notion, dependent on the very earthy assumptions of Jewish thinking, and underlined by the Christian belief about Jesus, that bodies could be raised from the dead.

Placing this reading with the two Old Testament lessons gives it the thrust of fear rather than of confrontation: how can we know that we shall be raised? Paul insists that, at the resurrection, change takes place. What is sown in one form, as seed, takes on new life as spirit.

The way to live with these complexities is to love our enemies. This is a tall order, for it requires not simply that we feel kind thoughts towards them – that would be difficult enough – but that we adopt a considered approach to them which will not let the desire for revenge gain the better of our conviction that people must live together in harmony.

A particular form of that conviction is contained in the final charge in this reading: do not pass judgment. Many of our statements in conversation and in secret are judgments of others. To what lengths of judgment do we often go, just in order to keep up with the crowd, or to justify ourselves or – simply out of anger – to put our neighbour down? A more profound set of values is being held up here than the simple pleasure of the immediate gratification of our rage.

What would it be to avoid passing judgment and to heap praise instead? Jesus suggests that, in the eternal scheme of things, we are subject to the same measure of judgment that we meet out to our neighbour. It could be that other people might become heaven, instead of hell, when we allow them to. There will be exceptions, of course, for this does not solve the Auschwitz problem. Some aspects of human behaviour cannot be brought within the bounds of comprehension, except in the fashioning of our own values.

*   *   *

The Second Sunday before Lent

Option A – Creation
Genesis 2:4b–9, 15–end
Psalm 65
Revelation 4
Luke 8:22–25

THE creation story told in Genesis 2 is probably older than the one found in Genesis 1; indeed, it may be part of the oldest strand of biblical tradition. It is not entirely consistent with the Genesis 1 account, either. The reader is told, 'In the day that the Lord God made the earth and the heavens ... then the Lord God formed man from the dust of the ground' – before he created all the other things on the earth. So much for seven days! God then created a garden, and the man was placed in it, 'to till it and keep it'; and he was given the freedom of all of it, except the 'tree of the knowledge of good and evil', on pain of death.

In this primal pastoral scene, with mists and water trickling through the tropes, the first human being was made factor, or manager, of God's estate; but he was lonely. So God created the animals – out of clay, just as man was made – and presented them to the man for naming. However, among them there could be found no helper equal to him, or appropriate for him. So God sent a deep sleep upon the man, and took one of his ribs and formed woman from it. The woman thus formed was therefore part of the man himself; so he clings to her, and they 'become' one flesh – again, we might think, since that it what they once were. This creation story ends in a celebration of marital love.

The praise of God the Creator is sung in Psalm 65 and in Revelation 4: 'By your strength you established the mountains'; 'You visit the earth and water it'; 'You crown the year with your bounty; your wagon trucks overflow with richness'; 'You are worthy, our Lord and God, to receive glory and honour and power, for you created all things, and by your will they existed and were created.' The emphasis is on the Creator rather than the Manager!

In Luke 8 the emphasis shifts again (or does it?) from the Creator to the human being on the earth – or water. Here, however, the man Jesus behaves in such a way as to demonstrate his power over the forces of evil. The creation story in Genesis 1 is represented as the triumph of God over nothingness, and here Jesus is shown as having power over the forces of evil which the sea represents. This is an exorcism; and it raises the question, Who is this man? – one which echoes other Gospels.

So we have jumped from creation to the question of the identity of Jesus. And that question is the lifelong concern of those who say they love him.

*   *   *

The Second Sunday before Lent

Option B
Sirach 27:4–7 *or* Isaiah 55:10–13
Psalm 92:1–4, 12–15
1 Corinthians 15:51–58
Luke 6:39–49

ONE commentator* says of the final verses in this passage from St Luke's Gospel: 'Implied in this is that the teaching of Jesus is never simply descriptive or informative, to which it is enough to be a disciple to give assent; it is always imperative, and assent consists in obedient action.' This parable concludes Luke's 'Sermon on the Plain', which in many respects is parallel to Matthew's 'Sermon on the Mount'. It is full of particular, detailed, moral instruction, principally about the danger that our lives may not submit to the judgment of their message.

If we were to be put on trial for our Christian faith, how much evidence would there be to convict us? Much of our time as Christian people is given to exploring the great teachings of our faith, such as, Who is Jesus? What kind of God do we believe in? What does the Church teach about the great ethical issues that our society faces? The assortment of instructions given in today's Gospel and in the reading from Sirach directs the moral focus to the minutiae of the believer's life-style. In the light of these two passages, we might consider the sobering thought that, whenever we open our mouths and speak, we provide evidence of the depth of our Christian discipleship.

The language of God might provide us with further food for thought. The prophecy in Isaiah 55 was probably written at about the time of the Israelites' return from exile in Babylon. The Lord has promised that their return shall happen, and it was part of the assumptions of ancient Israel that this very promise contained within it the seeds of its fulfilment. The prophet then speaks

---

* C. S. Evans, *Saint Luke. TPI New Testament Commentaries*, 1990, p. 340.

31

further of the reliability of God's word: it will not fail to achieve what it set out to accomplish. The people could look forward to their return journey across the desert to Jerusalem; the image is then of the very creation joining in their joyful homecoming. Such an event, says the prophet, will bring eternal honour to Israel's God.

St Paul looks forward to a different future: his vision of the final appearance of God. The imagery is drawn from the apocalyptic tradition of his day, and he is inspired by the thought of this imminent vindication of his ministry and of the endurance of his followers. The shortcomings and inadequacies of this life will be taken up and changed into imperishable glory; death will be destroyed, and Christ, already risen from the dead, and soon to be expected to set up the final reign of God, will be shown to be conqueror over all things.

Whatever our view of the end of the age – and we might have some difficulty with Paul's apocalyptic imagery – Christians believe that the future is in the hand of God, so whatever takes place will centre upon Christ and be open to the discovery of grace.

* * *

The Sunday before Lent

Option A – The Transfiguration
Exodus 34:29–35
Psalm 99
2 Corinthians 3:12 – 4:2
Luke 9:28–36 (*or* 28–43)

MOUNTAINS tend to be regarded as holy in most religious traditions, and Mount Sinai provided the scene for Moses' encounter with God to receive the Law. After this, the text of Exodus tells us, the skin of his face shone 'because he had been talking with God'. So intense was the brightness that a veil had to be placed over his face, so that he could address the Israelites.

St Paul uses this story to contrast the experience of those who are transfigured by the light of the gospel as they preach it. The Israelites may not have been able to see the face of Moses, but we are able to look on the face of Christ; they have their understanding veiled as they read the (Jewish) Law, he says, but we are able both to see clearly that its subject matter is Christ, and also to undergo the transformation which is brought about by the Spirit as we are changed into the likeness of Christ himself.

The pivot between the story of Moses and the interpretation of Paul is, of course, the Transfiguration story itself. Luke's version of the story represents a fascinating rewriting Mark's account. Luke tells us that it took place eight, not six, days after the preceding events; he specifically says that Jesus went up the mountain to pray, while Mark remains silent on this point; Luke draws immediate attention to Jesus' face, whereas Mark's emphasis is on his clothing; indeed, he does not use the verb 'transfigure', but merely says that Jesus' face 'was changed'.

Luke retains the connection, following Mark, with Jesus' prediction that 'there are some standing here who will not taste of death before they see the kingdom of God'. Whatever the reference of this statement was on the lips of Jesus, the kingdom of God, for the evangelists, is this event in the life of Jesus. Luke also gives an explicit reason for Jesus' ascent of the mountain – 'to pray' – and thus suggests that the experience might even be shared by disciples. Luke also keeps the main point of the story as the conversation of Jesus with Moses and Elijah, with Jesus himself left alone after the other two are removed from the scene. Peter's embarrassing exclamation is also retained, as is the connection with the baptism (by quoting the baptismal text, cf. Luke 3:22). However, the link with the resurrection is made more remote by the simple statement that the disciples told no one 'in those days' of what they saw and heard.

The subsequent story of the exorcism of the demon in Luke does not perform the same function as it does in Mark, either, for Luke leaves out the fact that the demon makes the boy deaf and dumb. This is important in Mark, for it draws together themes of understanding and speech which are not followed by Luke. Through all

33

the details of the textual differences between the Gospels, there is no doubt that we have here one of the most remarkable stories about Jesus. 'God became human,' wrote St Athanasius, 'in order that humanity might become divine.'

★   ★   ★

The Sunday before Lent

Option B
1 Kings 8:22–23, 41–43
Psalm 96:1–9
Galatians 1:1–12
Luke 7:1–10

How broad is the compassion of God in Christ? What limits are to be placed on God's reckless love for humanity? Today's readings are agreed that there are no limits, and that, as one hymn-writer put it, 'the love of God is broader than the measure of man's mind'.

Even the story of Solomon's dedication of the Temple around 952 BCE contains a reference to the possibility that people who are not members of the Israelite nation may come to it in order to pray, and Solomon's petition is that their prayers might be heard. The Psalmist rejoices in the greatness of Israel's God over all the idols – which are manufactured by their worshippers – 'but the Lord made the heavens'. So all nations are invited to worship him.

It is this universalist conviction that lay at the heart of Paul's missionary activity, and of his determination that access to Christ was not only through membership of the covenant people of God and commitment to the Jewish Law. To preach 'another gospel' – which is not really another, because it is not really good news – is to compromise the principle that all nations, all people, are invited to share in the blessings of the new covenant which is open to all in the person of Jesus Christ. Those who would dispute such an open and unconditional understanding of the good news of God in Jesus Christ are cursed, as far as Paul is concerned.

It is possible that his opponents were 'over-converted' Christians, who had heard of the Jewish heritage in which their faith started, and who wanted both themselves and other converts to share in all the details of the religion which formed the background to the new covenant in Christ. Paul will have none of this; the revelation of the gospel which he received from Jesus Christ was one which was for all, and his opponents' insistence upon observation of the Torah would compromise this universality.

A hint of God's complete impartiality is shown in the Gospel story in Luke. The centurion was a Gentile, and a member of the occupying force of Roman soldiers. However, he was locally regarded as a good man, for he had built a synagogue for the city, and was clearly compassionate towards his slave.

Jesus had no hesitation in granting his request, for he stands for the compassion of God, and 'the heart of the eternal is most wonderfully kind'. The centurion even becomes a sign to the Jews of their lack of faith in Jesus. It has recently been suggested that the slave may even have been the centurion's young sexual partner. If that is so, even further strains are placed upon *our* tendency to limit God's love.

*　　*　　*

Ash Wednesday

Joel 2:1–2, 12–17 *or* Isaiah 58:1–12
Psalm 51:1–17
2 Corinthians 5:20b – 6:10
Matthew 6:1–6, 16–20

HYPOCRITES are those who play-act. Religious people who feign 'goodness' may be said to have robbed God of the praise due to him. The readings at the beginning of the season of Lent call us to take off our costumes and our grease paint and to make changes in the way we live. We are to take a long hard look at who we have become, without make-up, so that in our turning towards Good Friday and Easter, it will be the goodness of God (rather than something phoney and less durable) which earths and energizes our journey.

The prophet Joel uses a plague of locusts as a dire warning of the judgment that will follow if the people do not change their ways. This may be a cryptic reference to the physical invasion of Israel. More likely the locusts are a device, symbolizing national disintegration, borrowed from the prophet Amos. They reiterate, in the fourth century BCE, a much older prophetic message: that repentance and prayer are the price of the Lord's continual toleration of a recalcitrant people. The oracle comes from a period of peaceful coexistence between religion and Persian domination, and the prophet alerts his contemporaries to the perennial danger of allowing an alien culture to set the agenda for God's people.

The reading from Isaiah is more specific. The practical needs of the post-exilic community provide the context for a call for justice for the hungry and the homeless. The emptiness of religious observance shows a wrong attitude towards God, who cannot be confined to any human institution. Both Joel and Isaiah warn us of the superficiality which can distort and enfeeble discipleship.

Whereas for Joel 'the day of the Lord' is a once-for-all and terrifying event in the future, for Paul it has already dawned. Jesus, God's anointed one, makes every day a day of salvation – a day in which to respond to God and to be grounded in the grace of God. Writing to the Corinthians, he tackles the thorny question of how to behave properly as Christian people, without play-acting. He reminds them that human inadequacy can block the transmission of grace, but insists that his own energy and perseverance in the face of difficulties are recognizable signs that he embodies 'the life of Jesus' (4:10–11). Tribulation strips off our theatrical garb and enables the life of faith to be lived at a level deeper than that of grease paint.

Almsgiving, prayer and fasting – three signs of a religious person – are all opportunities for 'play-acting' according to our gospel passage from Matthew. Applause is the actor's reward and is not a proper goal for those whose 'piety' should be directed solely towards God. The quest for applause, appropriate to an entertainer, perhaps, can never be the motivation for Christian disciples. They depend on the forgiveness of God and must receive that in a direct relationship with him, unalloyed by any limelight for themselves. The resources of faith lie in knowing ourselves loved and accepted, warts and all, by God alone.

* * *

The First Sunday of Lent

Deuteronomy 26:1–11
Psalm 91:1–2, 9–16
Romans 10:8b–13
Luke 4:1–13

CHRISTIAN discipleship means following Jesus into an encounter with evil, sometimes personalized in scripture as an autonomous devil. In today's readings this is explored at a number of levels. The concern in Deuteronomy for the care of outsiders is a reminder of how often the stranger is demonized to carry deep fears and prejudices. Israelite faith will incorporate 'the aliens who reside among you' within the community.

From a rather different perspective, Jesus is shown to be the fulfilment of the history of Israel, having a cosmic role in relation to evil. His followers are to recognize that even the roots of tragedy are within the very purpose of God as we experience it. The biblical tradition deals with this psychological reality in a number of ways, but contemporary insight supports the notion that suffering is neither a fate to be borne passively nor the ultimate enemy, but instead is a process of growth to which all are summoned.

The passage from Deuteronomy, describing a harvest pilgrimage, remembers the exodus from Egypt as the formative event that had called a people into being. 'A wandering Aramaean ...' stood at the centre of Israel's confession of faith from the beginning, and this invites us to trace our faith back to the experience of being foreigners, in the desert. It is a creed which incorporates the important insight, picked up in Luke's Gospel, that the wilderness is a place both of testing and of creative beginnings. In our thankfulness for nourishment and shelter, we are to remember not to externalize evil. Everything is grounded in God's love. God does not pull up evil by the roots, plead as we may, because the roots guarantee our freedom as we make our own desert journey.

In Paul's letters Jesus is often referred to as 'Lord', probably in answer to the many gods of the pagan religions. In this passage from Romans, God's powers and reign are exercised through Christ as God's representative, and things traditionally said about God may quite properly be said about Christ. In Paul's thinking the focus is on Jesus' stewardship of a ministry and mission delegated to him and shown in his life and death. The confession 'Jesus is Lord' is an individual commitment, and it is a lordship exercised over the Church corporately as well. Christian discipleship is always lived 'in the Lord' and, in New Testament terms, shares in the same cosmic conflict over which Jesus' ultimate and universal Lordship is assured.

The Gospel reading sets Jesus' earthly ministry in that cosmic context. Luke saw the whole life of Jesus as a life of temptation, which came to a head in the Passion. In the Bible this is the 'testing' of the true Son of God for his fidelity. The agent may be either God (as in the wilderness wanderings) or Satan (as in the story of Job). The immediate background for Luke's account is the wilderness temptations of Israel: Jesus succeeds where Israel fails (particularly in the supreme temptation of testing God) and so fulfils Israel's history.

It is on this larger canvas that Christian discipleship is to be understood. The call to 'embody Jesus' comes to the Church in barren and wilderness places, but the ultimate harvest is cosmic and universal. It offers a vision which beckons us towards a more humane world as we endeavour to live the struggle with sin and evil in ourselves and our communities. We are not 'like God, knowing good and evil' in any absolute or final sense.

*   *   *

The Second Sunday of Lent

Genesis 15
Psalm 27
Philippians 3:17 – 4:1
Luke 13:31–35 *or* Luke 9:28–36

TODAY'S exploration of discipleship is all about going beyond the vision, going beyond the known and the understood. Two Gospel passages share a common concern with Jesus' prophetic status. Both allude to his impending rejection and understand it as being within the divine purpose. Similarly, Paul, in writing to the Philippians, seems determined to counter any euphoric and triumphalist teaching by stressing the suffering he shares with Christ. In our passage he encourages his fellow Christians to follow this example.

The key factor in all this is that prayer lies at the heart of discipleship and may well represent the turning point towards suffering. Abram is viewed as the model for faith in the sense of responding with trust to what God offers. The Old Testament passage reaffirms two strands in God's promise to Abram: the first is that he will be the father of countless descendants, and the second is the gift of a holy land. But a brief comment by the narrator holds the key. Abram trusts God, and it is this attitude of prayerful commitment, and utter reliance going far beyond intellectual assent, which is the proper basis for facing whatever is to come. It is possible, perhaps necessary, to trust God in this way and yet live with very real uncertainties about the future. Such doubts are not the opposite of faith, but evidence of it. The final verse of Psalm 27 exhorts the disciple who prays and receives no answer to pray again and wait again in trust on the Holy One.

The theme of perseverance in the face of opposition continues as we move into the New Testament. Paul's relationship with the Philippians seems to have been a warm one. He wants to counter their spiritual enthusiasm with some earthy realism, hence the allusion to athletics to stress that the goal and transformation of Christians lies in the future. If there were Roman citizens in the congregation, the message would remind them that their citizenship of heaven takes precedence and will only be fulfilled with the return of the Lord Jesus.

The impression of a divinely destined itinerary, yet one that embraces earthly suffering, is reinforced in the passage from Luke 13. Nothing will stop Jesus' prophetic ministry short of its appointed end. If he is to die, it will not be at Herod's hands but within God's purpose. His journey, the pattern for Christian discipleship, also has its goal in the future. The story of the Transfiguration from Luke 9 provides another standpoint for understanding the coming rejection. The importance of Moses and Elijah underlines the focus on Jerusalem as the place both of suffering and of glory. Jesus, like them, is a supernatural figure and is fulfilling his divine destiny. Uniquely, the disciples are united with him in the cloud where they too have their call reaffirmed. They are the nucleus of the elect and are to receive his words as the words of God. In the face of his divinely certified suffering, Jesus is nevertheless momentarily shown to be what he will eventually become. The whole scene is set in the context of a time of prayer with a theme of faithful trust in God's purpose. Uncertainty about how this will be fulfilled is no bar to discipleship, and the inner three are summoned from the mountain down to the plain and onwards to the goal ahead.

*　　*　　*

The Third Sunday of Lent

Isaiah 55:1–9
Psalm 63:1–8
1 Corinthians 10:1–13
Luke 13:1–9

THE disciple is summoned to a life-change – otherwise known as 'repentance'. We are inclined to see this as an onerous demand, but today's readings – without underestimating the difficulty – emphasize the gracious invitation which the Church's penitential season represents. The word pictures range from rich banquets to wells of fresh water. These are contrasted with the sins and consequent disasters which deny access to these gifts.

The tone is set in the hymn from Isaiah which celebrates Israel's approaching restoration in terms very similar to Wisdom's invitation of Proverbs 9:1–6. The summons to a party includes the promise of pardon for all and a reminder that God who gives the pardon – and the party – may be found near at hand. The Psalm reiterates the theme of thirsting for God – a God who supplies our needs abundantly and whose grace is proffered to us as a free gift. The blessings of the past are renewed and set in a wider context. Israel's physical restoration is related to the restoration of her inner life, and this in turn is in response to a God who is central to the life of the whole world.

The New Testament reading continues the theme of water and nourishment. Here it is the Christian rites of baptism and Eucharist which, in Paul's view, are being idolized by the Corinthians, some of whom feel secure and complacent because they have these sacraments. Like the Israelites before them (who were lured into destruction) so the idolatry of the Corinthians will offer no guarantees against harm. The Christian life is lived by faith only.

The strange story of the barren fig tree continues the thought of impending destruction, and is at the same time the basis for a summons to a change of life. It picks up the images of thirst and nourishment in the gardener's appeal for a year's stay of execution for the tree, reminding us, perhaps, that the life of faith needs time and will not necessarily comply with our impatience. The rich manure of experience, sin and misadventure needs to be dug in and watered with tears of penitence before it will yield its fruits. But this is not simply an exhortation for individuals to repent of sin. It is also a prophetic warning that Israel as a nation is courting a disaster from which even religious people will not be exempt. Jesus' ministry offers the way forward for a whole society: our salvation is given to us corporately, inextricably bound up with changes in our common life. The party invitation is for everyone, and the people of God are summoned to make a life-change sustainable at national and global levels.

*   *   *

41

The Fourth Sunday of Lent

Joshua 5:9–12
Psalm 32
2 Corinthians 5:16–21
Luke 15:1–3, 11b–32

COMING home to a party in the land of promise and to the embrace of a loving father signals an uplifting and joyful experience. Today brings a different perspective to the Lenten encounter with evil and to the call to repentance. We are to turn round and see that we have crossed the river and that God has already surrounded us with loving acceptance. The image of a nourishing banquet, prepared for all, permeates the readings.

The passage from Joshua describes the keeping of Passover at Gilgal. The story follows on from the circumcision of a whole new generation of Israelites, a sign of their covenant with the God who has 'rolled away ... the disgrace of Egypt' and who now feeds them with the produce of the land of Canaan. God's people are not slaves but free agents. No longer must they eat manna in the wilderness; that debt is paid and they have come home to the land of promise. The Psalm, likewise, celebrates the joy of forgiveness – and of healing, commonly linked with it. The frail and wasted body will be sustained by nourishment and give evidence of God's favour.

In Jewish tradition neither sickness nor death was part of God's plan for humanity. This gets Paul into a fix when he comes to proclaim the gospel of Christ – since it is precisely the *death* of Jesus which he understands as effecting salvation. God's forgiveness reaches out to his creatures, but in their turn they have to renounce sin. Paul continues this appeal, reminding the Corinthians that assenting to the 'theory' is not sufficient – they should also conform to Christ in their behaviour. It will be their own freely-made decision which will reconcile them with God.

The story of the two brothers and their father is told in the context of a meal to two very separate groups of people. The 'tax collectors and sinners' are marginalized by Jewish society; and the 'scribes and Pharisees' believe themselves to *be* Jewish society. In this parable Jesus invites both groups to the banquet. The outcasts are to hear God's unconditional welcome and forgiveness; the 'righteous' may discover that, like the elder brother, they are in danger of excluding themselves from a continuous party. The freedom to refuse God's invitation to discipleship remains integral to the gift that is on offer. Human response and co-operation are won by love always – never by coercion. It is the younger son who, of his own volition, decides no longer to eat the filth to which his choices have led him, but to return and eat at his father's table.

* * *

The Fifth Sunday of Lent

Isaiah 43:16–21
Psalm 126
Philippians 3:4b–14
John 12:1–8

THE Lenten exploration of discipleship brings us to the threshold of Holy Week. The readings of this season have led inexorably towards the presentation of Jesus' passion as a triumphant climax to his healing and prophetic ministry. This is reinforced in John's Gospel where he is entirely in control of all that happens to him both before the trial (10:17) and during it ('you have no power over me', 19:11). The readings all focus on questions of identity. The little group of disciples, still on its way to Jerusalem, will be transformed into a community and empowered by Jesus' triumphant return to the Father. But first there is a dinner party. Here at Bethany, in his encounter with Mary and with Judas Iscariot, the matter of Jesus' identity comes to the fore as he is anointed king – a sign for his followers that God turns the world of appearances entirely upside down.

The reading from Isaiah 43 gives a similar sense of being on the brink of great salvific events. Again, the people who formed to declare God's praise stand on the threshold of a new identity. It is a work of God which fulfils a vision that can only be barely

43

glimpsed. It signals a change of fortune – the greening of the desert place. The Psalm intimates that the going out and returning home 'carrying sheaves' will nourish and sustain God's people. The Philippian church, in the New Testament, is similarly summoned to embrace a new calling. Paul is warning the church to beware of complacency and of putting confidence in religious institutions. He exhorts them to accept an identity as resurrection people, imitating himself: 'Forgetting what lies behind and straining forward to what lies ahead, I press on towards the goal for the prize of the heavenly call of God in Christ Jesus.'

In John's Gospel the crucifixion is set in the context of Passover celebrations. This gives Jesus' death a sacrificial significance. There is a sense of 'straining forward' towards the deliverance of God's people. Jesus will be 'enthroned' on the cross, so Mary's anointing is both a recognition of his royal dignity and an anticipation of his burial. Her own identity is not developed beyond this apparently unconscious prophetic act. By contrast, Judas is portrayed posturing behind a mask of piety. He knows the Law, but in his own dishonesty is resisting any true claim upon his life. Jesus' ministry as prophet and healer is reviewed and confirmed, and his new royal and priestly identity carries him forward 'towards the goal'.

* * *

Palm Sunday

Isaiah 50:4–9a
Psalm 31:9–16
Philippians 2:5–11
Luke 22:14–23, 56 *or* Luke 23:1–49

A WORLD turned upside down and a reversal of values have been features of the Lenten exploration of discipleship. The requirement of the followers of Jesus is that they live in counter-culture to their own society including, almost certainly, their religious institutions. On Palm Sunday the readings dramatize this topsy-turvy theme without flinching from the tragedy which it implies. For in Luke's Gospel Jesus is a tragic figure, and we have an opportunity to examine this today through three different accounts.

The first is the acclamation of Jesus by his disciples before he enters the city of Jerusalem. For the last time in Luke's Gospel, the Pharisees appear as their opponents. Even the stones of Jerusalem can recognize Jesus' royal status. It is quite simply rejected by the Jewish leaders. The second scene is Luke's account of the last supper, and here the emphasis is on the Messianic Banquet, where the destitute would enjoy whatever they lacked in this world. In an unjust society Jesus inaugurates a foretaste of paradise, where Christians are renewed as one body through participation in one loaf (1 Corinthians 10). He manages to emphasize both a physical satisfaction which is a present experience and also a perfect satisfaction in the next life. The echoes of Mary's Magnificat, in which the familiar world is turned upside down, ring through clearly. Thirdly, the Passion narrative from Luke expresses the rejection of God's chosen one by God's people, and reiterates the humiliation endured by Jesus, the one who should have been most honoured. It's a topsy-turvy world – and Luke is uniquely able to reinforce the evil of the moment because he will use a second volume to show how the Holy Spirit empowers the missionary work of the Church and vindicates the tragedy.

Confidence that God will reverse his fortunes – and the fortunes of Israel – is expressed by the servant in the Old Testament reading from Isaiah. The famous passage from Philippians describes Jesus in similar terms as a humble slave, obedient to the point of death, who is nevertheless exalted to the glory of God the Father. The power struggle between Paul and his Jewish Christian opponents, described in this letter, seems to have focused on the necessity for suffering – his own and that of Christ – in contrast to the complacency encouraged by his rivals. He goes on from this passage to spell out the implications for discipleship in terms of standing against the prevailing values: 'That you may be ... children of God without blemish in the midst of a crooked and perverse generation.'

The Monday of Holy Week

Isaiah 42:1–9
Psalm 36:5–11
Hebrews 9:11–15
John 12:1–11

PEOPLE with power like to hang on to it. We are all in danger of measuring our status in terms of the rewards that we receive. The Coronation service for a British monarch rightly emphasizes the responsibility of those with power to give service rather than receive it. When we proclaim Jesus as a 'king', all sorts of questions concerned with the use and abuse of such power immediately surface. It is a debate which lies at the heart of the Holy Week quest for Jesus' true identity. What we make of him – this week of all weeks – determines what we make of God.

Today the mood shifts noticeably from the innocent martyrdom of Luke's tragedy to the more regal preliminaries for 'enthronement' in John's Gospel. In full knowledge of a plot, Jesus returns to Bethany and is anointed by Mary 'six days before Passover'. This connection with Passover flags up the approaching sacrifice, while Jesus himself remains in control of all that happens. The threat to Lazarus' life is a reminder of the implications for faithful discipleship. We are offered an over-arching theme for the week: the anointing of Jesus as king already reinterprets tragedy – his burial and ours – in the light of future exaltation.

There can have been no more poignant tragedy for first-century Jewish Christians than the destruction of the Jerusalem Temple in 70 CE. The author of the letter to the Hebrews points to Jesus' enthronement as a sign that all sacrifice is now redundant. He reigns, not on the cross as in the Gospel, but in heaven – in the presence of God, a state promised to the faithful, which assures them of their salvation. Hebrews challenges all our attempts to localize God in our own religious institutions. Here the death and exaltation of Jesus is the replacement for Israel's previous means of access to God. His present enthronement in heaven has been achieved by faithful obedience. A death willingly accepted in obedience to the will of God is what makes his the superior

46

sacrifice. The superior sinlessness of Jesus lies in his life-long obedience to God which culminates in the cross. Hebrews is preoccupied with Jesus' present enthronement in heaven – achieved by faithful obedience. The gospel of human liberation means that everything else must serve that cause.

The Old Testament reading identifies the servant with Israel ('my chosen'), who will, with all patience, bring God's teaching and justice to the nations. The prophecies of Second Isaiah affirm that Israel – sometimes personified as prophet or king – will be exalted through suffering. When, in the Gospel, Mary anoints Jesus for his burial, it is the same kingdom of justice and freedom which is being announced. Jesus' royal identity, like that of the people of God, is the gift of God and bears fruit in service and in suffering.

* * *

The Tuesday of Holy Week

Isaiah 49:1–7
Psalm 71:1–14
1 Corinthians 1:18–31
John 12:20–36

THE present outbreak of ethnic conflicts indicates, as we know from history, that religion has its dark side. Genuine religion unites; distorted religion divides. The Holy Week quest for Jesus' true identity is continued in an exploration of light and darkness – a theme which will be pursued through the days leading up to his death. John's Gospel shows us the conflict in language normally reserved for apocalyptic 'end-time' events: it is as Son of Man that Jesus forms the connecting link between the earthly and heavenly spheres. His lifting up to die is also his exaltation in glory, enabling everyone (including Gentile Greeks) to be drawn to God. Meanwhile he remains hidden and unrecognized. This Gospel always shows Jesus as in command of the situation: characteristically the struggle with God over his destiny is resolved by divine affirmation almost before it is uttered.

47

Jesus' identity as Son of Man, explored in terms of light and darkness, has its mysterious side. Now you see him; now you don't. Jesus' future glory is visible to the eye of faith, but faith sees it most fully in darkness and suffering – thus it has ever been. The servant of the Lord is identified in Isaiah's prophecies with faithful Israel, and over the years has been applied to chosen individuals, so that the people of God may fulfil their destiny as 'light for the nations'.

Paul, in the first letter to the Corinthians, also sees the heart of the gospel in the cross of Jesus. Like John, he announces it as a mystery, as 'foolishness to those who are perishing'. The word 'wisdom' seems to have been misunderstood in Corinth. Paul allows it in 2:5, but prefers God's 'power' for the present. For Paul, the 'wisdom of God' is in direct conflict with the 'wisdom of the world' and is demonstrated above all in the folly of the cross. This is nothing to do with abstract or speculative thought, but more to do with recognizing God's authority and living in relationship with him. Closely associated with the work of God in creation, Wisdom in the Old Testament is the fulfilment of 'sensual' knowledge and exemplifies the biblical understanding of this relationship at its best. We fail to apprehend God in creation only because of our own self-regarding wisdom. Tempting the Lord – the sin of the desert (Numbers 14:11, 22) – implies a refusal to take God on trust and to worship our own image instead. Similarly, in the New Testament, the 'secret of the kingdom' is grasped by those on the edges – the Gentiles, the women, the socially or religiously marginalized – rather than by the disciples.

So, according to Paul, God's glory and wisdom remain hidden because human beings prefer to worship their own image. Jesus' mysterious identity, and the meaning of his death, elude definition. It is in his death that he returns to the Father. With apparent forethought and intention John refers to it in terms of the final victory at the end of time. It is left to his followers to realize the fullness of that victory. But first, recognizing that they walk in light, not darkness, they are to seek out the hidden wisdom – a means of new and relational experience for all God's people.

*　　*　　*

The Wednesday of Holy Week

Isaiah 50:4–9a
Psalm 70
Hebrews 12:1–3
John 13:21–32

A N exploration of Jesus' identity in terms of being both Son of Man and anointed King is now pursued in terms of Jesus as Prophet. This was the over-arching theme in Luke's Gospel: Jesus is the prophet destined to fulfil all prophecy. In John's Gospel it also has its place. Jesus reveals the Father, and those who witness this revelation choose either true or false discipleship. Again, Jesus is presented as being in control of the situation, as Lord of good and evil and of light and darkness. Today, with the prediction of his betrayal by Judas, the darkness of the night begins to close in ominously.

The reading from Isaiah describes the prophet pursuing his calling to 'sustain the weary with a word', while at the same time facing ridicule and judgment in a court of law. Confronting the adversary and the false friend in open trial adds a poignancy to the background to the Last Supper. God leads the servant safely through the darkness of rejection; by contrast, those who walk by their own lights will perish in the night. This may be extended to God's chosen people; both Israel and the Church are called to walk in the light and to project it into the darkness.

The author of Hebrews presents Jesus as a pioneer whose pilgrimage has brought him to the Promised Land of heaven where he is exalted to the right hand of God. He has gained access to the only sacred space worth having, so his friends should not hanker after alternatives such as the Jerusalem Temple. The passage is primarily an exhortation to perseverance, distinguishing between faithful precursors of faith (including Jesus) and the faithlessness of the wilderness wanderings. The exalted Christ is not a distant figure; his return is anticipated very soon.

John is preoccupied with Judas' treachery, and his fascination with the theme of loyalty and disloyalty suggests that he writes for a prophetic community threatened by outside pressures. Today it is a bitter betrayal of companionship which comes to the fore, but true friendship will also find its place in the story.

*   *   *

Maundy Thursday

Exodus 12:1–4 *or* 1–10, 11–14
Psalm 116:1–2, 12–19
1 Corinthians 11:23–26
John 13:1–17, 31b–35

OUR Holy Week exploration of who Jesus truly is reaches the heart of the matter with his presentation of himself as 'servant' and as 'teacher'. John's Gospel sets the killing of Jesus at the same time as the killing of sacrificial lambs for Passover, so this last meal with his friends is not the occasion for the institution of the Eucharist in this Gospel. Instead, an account of the foot-washing is included, and it is Jesus' self-sacrificing humility which is shown to us as an expression of his love for his friends. All the disciples save one are clean, and therefore fitted for Christ's service through their faith and loyalty. But even they who are already bathed must allow their feet to be washed. Forgiveness is the hallmark of the service which Jesus offers. True friendship and loyal discipleship are renewed by example.

The Exodus event was so crucial to the religion of Israel that it was used to inaugurate a new calendar and was commemorated with an annual festival. By the gracious action of God, an enslaved people was set free and led through the wilderness to the promised land. This deliverance is made present whenever the Passover is sacrificed and celebrated. The story is rehearsed in the present tense. Each generation makes it their own and it has upheld the Jewish people in every major crisis from that day to this.

Paul regarded Jesus as the new Christian Passover. For Jews, the Passover was and is the sacrifice and festival of God's deliverance, and for him Jesus has effected something similar. This is represented in the Last Supper which became the Christian memorial supper. Paul reinforces the connection between the supper and the death of Christ – for him the heart of the gospel. When Christians hold a common meal they recall aloud the event on which their existence is based. This recalling originally resembled the narration of the exodus from Egypt. The repetition is to continue until Jesus returns; and there can be little doubt that Paul expected this in his lifetime. The timescale gives an urgency and an immediacy to the narrative.

The quest for Jesus' true identity has almost reached its end. In John's Gospel the trial before Pilate brings it to a climax, but this supper scene lays a vital foundation: it is Jesus the servant and teacher who determines the character of the kingdom which he will inaugurate with his death. Without the example of self-giving love or the treachery of a friend, our own questions may well remain rather abstract. As it is, our search for God is to be earthed in human community.

* * *

Good Friday

Isaiah 52:13 – 53:12
Psalm 22
Hebrews 10:16–25 *or* Hebrews 4:14–16; 5:7–9
John 18:1—19:42

ON Good Friday the great themes of the penitential season all come together: hypocrisy is exposed, Jesus' identity is judged and the Roman governor is converted. The overwhelming message of the readings is that all who are oppressed, but who retain a sense that God is with them, will come to recognize how little jurisdiction any worldly authority really has. There is an exploration of what it means to move in and out of a sense of God's presence.

The servant – originally, perhaps, the imprisoned king or victimized prophet – is also to be understood as the suffering and exiled people of God. In many ways this 'Song of the Servant' is a Passion narrative with which it is easier to identify than the triumphant portrait of Jesus in John's Gospel. Constantly worked over through hundreds of years, it is able to interpret both personal and national events with power and poignancy. The Psalmist, similarly, is a person of influence and authority in an unexpected situation of helplessness. Psalm 22 is, after all, ascribed to King David! There is raw emotion in the language; the Psalmist 'roars' like a lion in his anger and bewilderment (v. 1), and there is a grandiose dimension in the powerful animals and the call to all the nations. The central issue is trust in God. The Psalmist feels utterly betrayed, and there is a bitter contrast between the religious language of God's *presence* and the powerful experience of God's *distance* in his time of need: 'My God! My God, why ...?'

The movement from distance to presence – and endurance for the task – is a dominant motif in Hebrews. An appeal to God's faithfulness is the basis to a call for similar faithfulness on the part of the Christian group which is being addressed. The attainment of God's purposes always lies in the future – only Jesus has already entered his presence, but Christians are encouraged to follow him as they approach heaven themselves. The bar to access is guilt, and it is the author's conviction that this has been removed through the sacrifice of Christ. Jesus' suffering and humanity are the source of his effectiveness as 'priest', but it is to his exaltation that Christians are to look for encouragement. The notion of perfection and sinlessness is best understood in the context of the Day of Atonement rituals, in which sacrifice was integral to the process. It is by his sacrifice that Jesus attains heaven, the true Holy of Holies. In death he is, by this analogy, both priest and victim. Primarily, however, he is God's unique and obedient Son – in the traditional Jewish understanding of suffering as God's disciplining of his children. Hebrews concentrates on the effect rather than the cause of the crucifixion, and so has no need to stress the injustice of the cross. Unlike today's Gospel Passion narrative, for this author sacrifice and exaltation are not fused but are two separate acts.

In John's Gospel, the Jerusalem authorities have tried to seize or kill Jesus several times. In the face of this hostility he sets the sovereign tone early on: 'I lay down my life ... I lay it down of my own accord' (10:17). It is those who come to arrest him who fall back to the ground, helpless. The trial scene is more a judgment of Pilate than of Jesus, and the burial is that of a king who has ruled from the cross. All in all it is a story seen with the eyes of faith. But, within it, there is a narrative of Pilate moving from incomprehension and fear to an extraordinary acknowledgement of Jesus' power and authority. Typical of John is the constant movement of the Roman governor in and out of his palace. There is indecision, the attempt to do the right thing, weakness and ignorance. One man's struggle with unbelief and his conscience (occasionally echoed in the behaviour of Peter the disciple) gives texture to the message that an apparent distance from God's love may paradoxically be a place of conversion, the discovery of God's nearer presence.

* * *

Easter Eve

Job 14:1–14 *or* Lamentations 3:1–9, 19–24
Psalm 31:1–4, 15–16
1 Peter 4:1–8
Matthew 27:57–66 *or* John 19:38–42

THE mood of today's readings follows the events described in the gospel. From Matthew's account there is finality, sadness and an affirmation of God's constancy but little assurance for the future. From John's account there is the grandeur of a royal burial, but it is somewhat anti-climactic after the enthronement and exaltation of the king on the cross. The story of Jesus' burial meets Christians in a place of confused anticipation, and the other readings echo both the hope and the bereavement.

Lamentations and Job date from the period of the exile. Job seems to be addressed to those in captivity, but Lamentations is aimed at those who remained amongst the ruins. The sufferings of Judah are described and attributed to the direct activity of God's judgment. So bitter was the anguish and so oppressive the burden that the author could not banish it from his thoughts. Only the realization that the long-overdue penitence was now clearly evident enabled him to hold out any hope at all for the future. Both authors give magnificent expressions of faith in the covenant mercies of God, and are able to look to the distant future with renewed optimism.

The first letter of Peter portrays Jesus as the new Enoch who, in Jewish apocalyptic tradition, visited the underworld to seal the doom of all the evil powers associated with Satan. The main reason for the letter is to encourage an isolated Christian group in their discipleship, so this assurance of God's overall control is well suited to their situation. It finds an echo whenever people feel at the mercy of ruthless forces, and 'he descended into hell' survives today in the Apostles Creed. What may have begun in 1 Peter as a way to emphasize Jesus' identification with the human lot was expanded to hold out the hope that all are within the scope of salvation. The letter itself is not so positive about universal salvation and warns readers against the temptation to avoid suffering by assimilating to alien ways.

All the Gospels attribute Jesus' burial to Joseph. Matthew's narrative particularly leaves us in no doubt that Jesus really died and was buried. It reminds readers of the suffering servant of Isaiah, and the setting of the guard alerts them to a possible but false explanation of the empty tomb. Matthew writes to convince us that Jesus was indeed the one promised by God in scripture. He seems to have known that his readers would be confronted with Jewish criticism of Jesus as a magician and deceiver; he tackles the sceptics head-on. John make rather more of Joseph and Nicodemus who, in his Gospel account, believe 'secretly' until this moment. Now they come publicly – in the light – as all believers must. There has been a gradual conversion – a movement, like that of Pontius Pilate, towards discipleship. This may be an encouragement to other synagogue leaders to follow the same way. Like Pilate they seem to acknowledge Jesus as king, using the huge amounts of spices associated with royal burials and giving him a garden sepulchre like that associated with King David.

Jesus' burial, like all burials, faces us with our mortality. It makes us sad; but, as often happens, it is loss which brings us up short and enables us to stop hedging our bets and to live fearlessly with our true choices. Joseph and Nicodemus offer a model of faith for the cautious and sceptical of every age.

★   ★   ★

Easter Day

The Principal Service
Acts 10:34–43 *or* Isaiah 65:17–25
Psalm 118:1–2, 14–24
1 Corinthians 15:19–26 *or* Acts 10:34–43
John 20:1–18 *or* Luke 24:1–12

IT is entirely appropriate that a kaleidoscope of themes should be present in the readings for this day, the most important in the Christian year, when the whole spectrum of believing is brought into the focus of our vision of Jesus, the crucified, now raised from the dead.

The reading from the penultimate chapter of the book of Isaiah belongs to the third section of that prophecy, and it deals with the hope, on the part of those who have returned from exile, that God will accomplish new things for Jerusalem. The picture painted is almost utopian, with no violence, no natural disasters and no family sadnesses; even the animals will cease to feed off one another.

The Psalmist in Psalm 118 celebrates the king's entry into the Temple at the autumn festival. He experiences a ritual humiliation in order to know a triumphant glorification; and in doing so he embodies the life of his people. He feels the pain of rejection, but exults in the joy of restoration – like a stone at first rejected by the builders but now made into the most significant in the building.

These themes of the new age and of glorious renewal naturally echo Christian joy at the resurrection of Jesus. His new life is the life of the new age which God inaugurates when he establishes his final kingdom; and where he reigns in resurrected glory, there is

55

peace among the whole of creation. St Paul is expressing this connection when he speaks of a hope which extends beyond this world to the age to come. For him, as well as for all the earliest disciples, the resurrection of Jesus marked the start of the coming of the end, when God would return to vindicate his people and establish his kingdom on earth. St Peter's experience draws different implications from the story; his decision to baptize Gentiles expressed his sense of God's call to all people for inclusion in the divine purposes.

All this – and more – derives from these simple yet complex stories of a group of women – or one woman! – going to the tomb of Jesus on the third day after his crucifixion and finding that his body was no longer there. Our choice of Gospel reading will determine the flavour of the story we hear. St Luke tells of a group of women, three of whom he names, whose perplexity turns to recall of the words of Jesus and joyful spreading of the news. The focus then switches to Peter, who looks in and sees the linen cloths and returns home 'amazed'.

St John's is a more personal and 'romantic' version of the story. Peter's run becomes a race with the 'disciple whom Jesus loved', who outruns him; nevertheless it is Peter who enters the tomb first. It has been suggested that the disciple whom Jesus loved represents the 'ideal' disciple, whether an historical figure or not, whom St John portrays as close to Jesus in his trials, and the first to believe in his resurrection. The focus then shifts to Mary Magdalene. All we are told of her in the New Testament is that she was at the tomb on the morning of the resurrection, ready to anoint the body of Jesus, and that, according to Luke 8:2, 'seven demons had gone out' from her. This tradition is repeated in the 'shorter ending' in Mark 16:9, with the additional information that it was Jesus who had cast them out. Her touching story has provided imagery for all who at first have not seen, but whose weeping has been turned to joy when they have been addressed by the risen Lord.

*   *   *

Easter Day

Eucharist late in the day
Isaiah 25:6–9
Psalm 114
1 Corinthians 5:6b–8
Luke 24:13–49

ISAIAH 25 begins a section of respite after some stinging oracles of judgment in the previous chapters. Here the prophet looks to the future and sees the Lord preparing for all nations 'a feast of rich food, a feast of well-aged wines'. The prophet is looking forward to happier times for God's people, when God will welcome all people to his table, and the restored fortunes of Judah will be a metaphor for the condition of the human race.

In Psalm 114 the image of escape from slavery in Egypt is a powerful one for a nation which has also known exile in Babylon. The images of those historical events merge in the poet's mind, with the Red Sea looking back and fleeing, just as in Exodus 14; the River Jordan turning back, as in Joshua 3; and the mountains of the Fertile Cresent 'skipping like rams' as the returning exiles cross the desert from Babylon. In these few verses is recounted the saving history of Israel.

These images of escape, deliverance and rejoicing hover in the background of Christian meditation on the resurrection of Jesus. The reader of Luke 24 knows what the participants in the story do not: that it was 'Jesus himself [who] came near and went with them'. This irony keeps the story going until the moment of recognition. His question 'What things?' comes from the lips of a skilful listener, who, knowing the whole story, knows also that it is important for the distressed to recount it in their own words. So the grief is poured out, and the wise counsellor invites the sad disciples to consider the texts of scripture which can give meaning to their pain. When the conversation ends they are hungry for more, and this hunger provides the opportunity for the disclosure of the stranger's identity; 'made known to them in the breaking of the bread'.

That is the way in which the Lord God 'wipes away the tears from all faces'; by accompanying on the road, by eliciting the story, by comparing it with scripture, by agreeing to stay in the company of those who need him, and finally by making himself known in the ordinary event – eating – which is transfigured into the extraordinary – the Christian Eucharist.

To live in the light of the resurrection is not principally to enjoy ecstatic experiences, however. It is to be holy and righteous. We can read the passage from 1 Corinthians as a salutary warning which, though concerned with bread, makes a point that depends upon the imagery of bread which is unleavened. St Paul points to the fact that yeast is present throughout the dough, and he takes it as a metaphor for what is old and needs clearing away. To make bread, the cook needs to keep a piece of bread with live yeast from yesterday's batch; at Passover time, all the yeast is cleared out of the house, so that only unleavened bread can be made. Christ, 'our Passover', makes for a new life, with the old tendencies to decay removed. St Paul wants the Easter celebration to reflect the fact that those who have been renewed by the resurrection of Christ have done away with 'malice and evil' and are living lives of 'sincerity and truth'.

* * *

The Second Sunday of Easter

Acts 5:27–32
Psalm 118:14–29 *or* Psalm 150
Revelation 1:4–8
John 20:19–31

THERE is a sense in which it is curious that there should be any 'Easter Sunday' and 'Sundays of Easter' at all, for *every* Sunday is the festival of Easter; the celebration of the living presence of Jesus is not restricted to an annual festival. However, the same might be said against its observance every week; why not a reminder of and thanksgiving for the resurrection of Jesus every day?

This is where Christian living and prayer come in. The life of the earliest church was, we are told, characterized by boldness, confidence, praise and peace, and these are marks both of Christian living and of Christian praying.

The Acts of the Apostles provide us with a defence of the early Christian community before the Roman authorities; these are no troublemakers, but loyal, devout members of society, who want to have the freedom to worship and to go about their business as believers in the risen Jesus. When this life-style conflicts with the demands of the authorities, then they are prepared to stand their ground and defend their position with boldness.

A different kind of boldness, or confidence, is what marks Psalm 118. Here the praying community expresses its confidence in the victory of God. Psalm 150 gives no particular reason for praise, it just gets on with it. Lovers don't keep asking why they are loved, they rejoice in the knowledge that they are.

At the root of all this confidence and praise is the story of the presence of Jesus. Thomas had been absent when the risen Lord had shown himself to the disciples on the evening of the resurrection. This detail of the earlier story makes possible the statement which applies to all of us who have believed in Jesus since those earliest days: 'Blessed are those who have not seen and yet believe!' The gift of the peace of Christ is the constant factor between those days and our own; to know him is to love him, and to love him is to know ourselves already loved by God, his Father and ours.

To these stories are added the opening story from the Book of Revelation concerning John's call to write the vision which he saw. The impetus to writing was provided by the same Spirit who raised Jesus from the dead and who inspires the Christian life of prayer and confidence.

*　　*　　*

59

The Third Sunday of Easter

Acts 9:1–6 *or* Acts 9:1–20
Psalm 30
Revelation 5:11–14
John 21:1–19

WHATEVER else the resurrection is about, it certainly is to do with new beginnings. Today's readings speak of two such beginnings.

The call of St Paul has become a classic narrative of our civilization. A 'Damascus Road' experience is a symbol of conversion, of repentance, of a change of mind. The details of the story are etched in our memories. We have all stood by as Paul is blinded; we have looked with Paul on the inside of our eyelids and seen the darkness; we have felt the hesitation of Ananias; we have felt moved at this one disciple's obedience; we have wept with joy at this turning to God on the part of a former persecutor, who became such a formidable propagandist; and we have also remembered the warning, 'I myself will show him how much he must suffer for the sake of my name'.

This is a story of what happened when one person was confronted by the living Christ. Something happens which can only generate the language of newness. But at the centre of that newness remains the image of crucifixion, for this is how the newness is brought about; the freshness of resurrection life is purchased at the cost of sacrificial love. So there is a connection between the self-disclosure of Jesus as 'the one whom you are persecuting' and his promise to Ananias: 'I myself will show him how much he must suffer for the sake of my name.' The servant will not be above his Master. These are the grounds for praise at the vision of God in the Book of Revelation. It is the Lamb who was slain who is accounted worthy to receive 'power and wealth and wisdom and might and honour and glory and blessing'.

The new beginning of the disciples in the Gospel is the same as Paul's, but different. Here are disciples who have known the Lord in his earthly life. Is Peter's decision to go fishing a sign of lack of

60

faith, a desire to return to the old ways, a hankering for the days before the Lord came and interrupted his life, or is it motivated simply by the need to eat? Its importance in the story is that it sets up the possibility of an encounter with Jesus; whatever it was, it provides the context in which Jesus shows himself again and renews his love and trust in Peter.

Both the completely new and the renewed have their place in the mission of God; and both 'newnesses' have their origin in the resurrection of Jesus, with whom every day is a new beginning, every fall a new start, and every mistake the opportunity to be rescued.

Psalm 30 could have been written for these disciples. The misplaced zeal which led one to persecute and the other to deny or flee; the blindness which afflicted Paul in the process of his conversation; the sad resignation in Peter's 'I'm going fishing': all these were grounds for self-questioning and confusion; but God, 'rich in mercy', restores them to life 'from among those gone down to the Pit'.

* * *

The Fourth Sunday of Easter

Acts 9:36–43
Psalm 23
Revelation 7:9–17
John 10:22–30

THE reader of the Acts of the Apostles over these weeks may be struck by how the early Christian community lived the resurrection faith. The reference in this story to the 'saints and widows' suggests a community which has been in existence for a period of time, with some structure to its life. 'The saints' was a term for the whole community, and 'the widows' were probably those given the task of grieving with the families of the dead – much like the mourners in the story of Jairus' daughter in Luke 8:41ff. This suggests that, according to Luke – who also wrote the Acts of the

Apostles – their life was, on this occasion, punctuated by a repetition of the Easter story.

The other readings carry the theme of 'comfort' in adversity. In the case of Psalm 23 this is a general theme, but the others have added sense of comfort in tribulation for disciples who suffer persecution. The seer in Revelation 7 learns of those 'which are come out of great tribulation', and John 10 speaks of the safety of those who are Jesus' sheep. That this part of the Gospel narrative takes place at winter adds significance to the protection that is offered to the sheep. They will not perish because they are protected both by the Son, who is the 'good shepherd', and by the Father, whose purpose is to keep faith with the Son.

The implication is, first, that tribulation is bound to come, but that, second, those who suffer will be consoled by Jesus himself and his Father. Few Christians in the West can be said to suffer much by way of 'tribulation' now. However, we do well to remember that many Christians in the past have done so, and that many still do in different parts of the world. We also know now that Christians have not only been persecuted, but also have carried out persecutions; and we know too that people suffer unjustly simply for believing in something which is not acceptable to those in authority, or for acting on behalf of justice for those who suffer oppression.

Clearly, the point of the biblical exhortations to constancy are that God is on the side of his own people. The corollary today, as we consider who are God's people, must surely be that Christ is to be known in all the persecuted men, women and children around the world, and that God is on the side of the victims. A contemporary resurrection faith will therefore suggest that vindication comes not simply to those who are Christians, but that God's purposes are focused in those who suffer for the cause of righteousness, and for those who are widowed and orphaned by the injustice of oppressors.

★ ★ ★

The Fifth Sunday of Easter

Acts 11:1–18
Psalm 148
Revelation 21:1–6
John 13:31–35

How wide is the love of God? Who is saved? Today's readings provide a biblical pattern for an understanding of human salvation that gradually widens, till all people are included. The continuing story from the Acts of the Apostles is of Peter's defence of himself before the church in Jerusalem. The baptism of Cornelius in Acts 10 had marked a watershed in the life of the early Christian community. Before then, the young church believed that belief in Jesus was simply one form of Jewish faith, of which there were several versions available. Peter's experience of God's leading convinced him, however, that Gentiles should also be admitted to faith. A little later, of course, Paul arrived on the scene and took an even more radical view of the implications for the whole human race of the life, death and resurrection of Jesus. Peter's account was accepted, we are told here, and the community gave thanks for God's ever-widening mercy, in that Gentiles were to be admitted to the fellowship of Christ's Church.

So the Bible marks the early stages of this development in human religious understanding, and provides some means of establishing criteria by which we construe what is compatible with faith in Christ. Here we see the beginnings of the development of the divine purpose of human salvation, through the chosen people of Israel, through the Church, through all people who respond, in sometimes unknown and hidden ways, to the God who is revealed in Christ. Psalm 148 has the Psalmist calling upon the whole creation to give thanks for the glory of God, especially in his concern for his people, and with the New Testament's gloss on the meaning of Israel, we may see this as referring to the whole human race.

The same theme is present in the Gospel. Jesus' exclamation, 'Now the Son of Man has been glorified, and God has been glorified in him', occurs after Gentiles have approached the disciples with the desire to see Jesus. There is this thrust implicit in the Christian gospel for the uniting of the whole of humanity, and it is significant that such a weighty theological theme should issue, in John's Gospel, in Jesus giving a 'new commandment': that his followers should love one another. The unity which Christ desires and which is central to Christian preaching comes to expression in simple obedience; that those who take any note of him should live as he lived – in love. The glory of Christ is the love of people for one another. In that way they show that they have his spirit.

★ ★ ★

The Sixth Sunday of Easter

Acts 16:9–15
Psalm 67
Revelation 21:10; 21:22 – 22:5
John 14:23–29 *or* John 5:1–9

Two Gospel readings are provided for today. The passage from John 14 is prefaced by the question from Judas (not Iscariot, we are told; this is no trick question from a future betrayer): 'Lord, how is it that you will reveal yourself to us, and not to the world?' Jesus ignores the question and speaks of the love which is to reign in the Christian community. He talks, too, of the peace which he will leave as he departs from them. St John, of course, has no account of the Ascension, the festival which takes place this coming week. When Jesus talks of his departure, then, he is referring to his crucifixion and resurrection and his eternal presence with his disciples by the Spirit. With Jesus no longer physically present among the disciples, it is important that they remember the promise of his spiritual presence.

The Gospel reading from John 5 is about conflict: the words, 'Now that day was a sabbath', are the clue to that. The fact that the pool by the Sheep Gate had five porticos suggests that it was constructed to reflect the five books of the Law of Moses – the 'Pentateuch', as we call the first five books of the Jewish scriptures. In Jewish tradition, this Law taught the people how they were to conduct themselves – or 'walk', to use the metaphor which translates the Hebrew word *halakah*. After ensuring that the man who has been ill for thirty-eight years names his own need, Jesus instructs him to take up his mat and 'walk'. The story proceeds with the conflict that ensues as the man, cut loose from the 'walk' of his former religious tradition, obeys the command of Jesus and gets into trouble with those who are supposed to be guiding the people in their walk before God. (There are salutary lessons here for those of us who claim to be teachers of the faith.)

In the order in which we read these lessons, the vision of new Jerusalem sets the scene for this encounter of Jesus with the people and authorities of the earthly Jerusalem. The nations are to 'walk' in the new holy city, and kings and peoples shall acknowledge its priority in glory and honour. The city is lit by the Lamb of God, and has need of no other light, so none will stumble; this will be home to all, and everything which would defile it is excluded.

So we come back to Philippi, the first city in which Paul preached the gospel in Europe. Here there was a prayer meeting, and a faithful woman who welcomed the apostles into her home. So a seller of purple cloth, the fabric of royalty, welcomes the ambassadors of the king of kings, and is numbered among those who will inherit and walk the streets of the city which is to come.

* * *

Ascension Day

Acts 1:1–11
Psalm 47 *or* Psalm 93
Ephesians 1:15–23
Luke 24:44–53

How do you tell the story of the end of the life of Jesus? Usually, the story of somebody's life ends with their death; but, of course, the most important statement about Jesus is that he is not dead, but risen from the dead. Each evangelist tells his story differently. Mark's account hardly has a proper resurrection, because there are no appearances to disciples. Matthew and John describe him not going away at all but, in ways that are neither explained nor explored, staying with the disciples and continuing, as the risen Son of God, to share their common life. Luke is the evangelist most committed to story-telling. He looks out for the causes and the effects of things, and makes theories and ideas into narratives.

Most of the best stories about Jesus come from Luke. The shepherds at his birth; the chorus of the angels; the stories of Elizabeth and Zacharias; some of the best known parables – such as the lost coin, the lost sheep and the prodigal son. What is more, Luke is the only evangelist to offer us a 'volume 2', the Acts of the Apostles, which carries the story of the followers of Jesus on into the life of the earliest churches.

For Luke, the life of Jesus consists in his preaching of the kingdom of God, which includes all people in God's compassionate and barrier-free reign. Jesus' death represents the *apparent* triumph of the forces of evil, but in fact is all part of God's plan for the salvation of all, for it issues in the raising of Jesus from the dead. The stories of Ascension and Pentecost are expansions of the resurrection story; they are particular types of resurrection appearances; the Ascension explains why the resurrection appearances ended, and Pentecost says how Jesus is still present to his disciples. Luke tells of the end of the appearances in order to show that Jesus had gone to share in the life of God.

So there is a second question: why were the disciples not sad when he left them? They are in John 16, but Luke seems more confident of what he is doing: that is, preparing the narrative ground for the story of the coming of the Spirit. The Ascension story is Luke's way of understanding the resurrection; it is not an absence, but it paves the way for a newly understood presence.

Luke's story says he goes away – as the story must, for the resurrection appearances of Jesus have stopped. But this is in order to make way for the story of the coming of the Spirit. This is not necessary in Matthew, for Jesus remains present. So in Luke there is a narrative paradox in order to allow for a theological statement.

The point is, of course, that this is not a physical 'going' to another place, for God's home is not a place. God the Father lives everywhere by the Spirit. Jesus' 'going to the Father' necessarily implies and entails that his disciples 'go to the Father' with him – even though Luke tells us this as having God come to them, as the Spirit. Hence the disciples' joy. They know that they are joined with Christ as he goes on to his future in the life of the Church. They also know that the kingdom of God really has dawned among them. All people are now made one with Christ, 'outsiders' and all!

The ascension of Jesus is the ascension of the whole of humanity to share in the life of God. That is the destiny of humankind; that is the presence of the kingdom of God, and that is what Christ brings about – he is both means and reality. This is cause for great thanksgiving and praise. So the Psalms we sing today are appropriately that of God's kingship, for it is a kingship in which Jesus shares, along with all who are called to reign with him.

★   ★   ★

The Seventh Sunday of Easter

Acts 16:16–34
Psalm 97
Revelation 22:12–14, 16–17, 20–21
John 17:20–26

IN between the celebrations of Ascension and Pentecost, the Gospel draws our attention to what is commonly known as the 'High Priestly' prayer of Jesus in John 17. This remarkable composition is not a proof text for ecumenism, but a prayer for something more profound. It was, of course, penned before there were any structural divisions in the Church, so it represents a desire for a unity which is nothing to do with ecclesiastical organization. We do well to note that the model for which the unity is prayed is that which exists between the Father and the Son – indeed, that which existed 'before the foundation of the world'. It also makes a particular reference to those who believe after the time of the apostles – and that includes us modern readers, so it clearly originates in a time and place which no longer thought of the end of time as imminent!

How is it to be understood? What is that unity which Jesus eternally enjoys with the Father? The word used in this passage is 'love'. Elsewhere in John's Gospel the suggestion is made that the love between Jesus and the Father is evidenced in their wanting the same thing, in their working towards the same ends, in their having the same purpose. That purpose is the salvation of the world, and its effects are to be seen in the love which human beings have for one another.

Those who have this hope find no difficulty in proclaiming, 'The Lord is king! Let the earth rejoice; let the many coastlands be glad!' Paul and Silas were singing the praises of God when the opportunity came to escape from prison in Philippi. Their refusal to do so led to the conversion of their jailer and his whole household. (They did not simply rejoice that the jailer had become a believer, as the New Revised Standard Version suggests; rather, that the whole household was baptized.) The feast prepared for Paul and Silas was a precursor of the wedding breakfast of the Lamb to which all are invited to share in their passion for doing the will of God. The Book of Revelation rightly finishes on a note of celebration.

* * *

Pentecost

Acts 2:1–21 *or* Genesis 11:1–9
Psalm 104:24–35b
Romans 8:14–17 *or* Acts 2:1–21
John 14:8–17, (25–27)

IT seems that our prayers are frequently answered by all the ambiguity which met Philip's request for more specific information about how Jesus relates to the Father. Why could he not be more specific: We have to look at the evidence around us and decide that the God who is the Father of Jesus is the God who is worthy of our worship. In order to know the answer, it would appear that we have to commit ourselves to the loving life-style of the God who is known to us in Jesus: 'If you love me, you will keep my commandments, and I will ask the Father, and he will give you another Advocate, to be with you forever. This is the Spirit of truth ...' Yet again, we are being told that to know God is to act like God in love and compassion.

The lectionary is absolutely right to place the story of the Tower of Babel alongside the story of Pentecost. Babel, or Babylon, of course, stood for all that was evil in the eyes of Jewish tradition, and the name of the city which dared to vie with God in glory was given also to that prehistoric society representing a human race which attempted to build a tower to reach to the heavens; there is a play on the word *babel*, which has connotations of confusion, for the punishment for this presumption was the confusion of their language. The Acts story reverses the judgment, and tells of nations formerly divided by language now brought together by the Spirit of God; all those visitors to Jerusalem heard the disciples speaking in their own tongue. Luke's theological creativity brings these two stories together and makes a point about the significance of language and speech, especially with regard to the preaching of the good news of Jesus Christ.

In the reading from Romans, Paul tells of the Spirit which is given to Christian believers. This is none other, he says, than the Spirit which is at work in creation; this is not some extra special attribute of God, but God at his creative work. There are no distinctions to be drawn between the various works of God. God creates, God judges, God reconciles; all is the work of the one God. It is the Spirit of God who undertakes all that God wills, and it is the grace of God which underlies all God's actions. This Spirit makes us the children of God, the inheritors of the estate. The one proviso is that we remember the cost of this grace to God, bearing in mind that what we suffer is also to be offered to the Father to be made holy, just as was the offering of Christ himself.

* * *

Trinity Sunday

Proverbs 8:1–4, 22–31
Psalm 8
Romans 5:1–5
John 16:12–15

A familiar picture seen in a gallery or a favourite novel re-read –
both ask us to take a breathing space so that we can reassess
their impact. Trinity Sunday gives us the chance to take a step
back from the life story of Jesus of Nazareth, which we have been
following for the last few months, and to consider the difference
which that story has made to the way in which we view the world.

A tone of interconnectedness is set in the first reading from
Proverbs. Wisdom, in the biblical tradition, is not thought of
primarily as abstract knowledge or speculation, but as personal and
moral knowledge. To 'know God' is to recognize his authority
and live accordingly. Here Wisdom is a female principle who
actively seeks out those who will listen to her. Like the Logos in
John's Gospel, she reveals the secrets of God to those who will
accept her. Closely associated with the work of God in creation,
she is the fulfilment of all 'natural' knowledge. If Jesus shows us the
'wisdom' of God then we are reminded to look for him in
mundane material.

The theme of a good and interconnected universe is continued in
Psalm 8. Stepping back from the picture shows us the broader
canvas, enabling us to see more of the grand design and to be awed
by the scale of it. If we are to see our calling to full humanity in the
life story of Jesus, then there is something here about perspective.
In the peculiarity and particularity of the apparently insignificant,
the majestic work of God goes on.

Paul, writing to the Romans, is anxious not to be misunderstood.
He believes that salvation is assured for those in Christ, but does
not believe that the resurrection life is yet attained in its fullness.
On the basis of God's gracious initiative much is achieved, and the
life of the Holy Spirit is poured out, but there is still work to be
done; and Christians, humbled by their afflictions, are to put their
trust in God and not in themselves. As we step back from the

grand canvas we may be given a glimpse of how our own brush-strokes can be incorporated – of how unlikely colours may yet be included. The life story of Jesus has shown us that human limitation does not constrain God.

The reading from John's Gospel is a reminder not to allow our images of God to become static. For this evangelist the Spirit is the Spirit of Truth – and 'truth' is one of his key words. Truth lies in the future and allows the possibility of some surprises yet to come. In this last gift of Jesus to his disciples we are encouraged to keep moving. If we continue to be his disciples, and from time to time to reassess the impact of his life story, we shall be gradually caught up in the dynamic of God's love and the whole picture will swirl with the divine life which he shows us.

*   *   *

The Sundays after Trinity

Please see Table on p. 125 for the date of First Sunday after Trinity and the Proper to use for the year.

– Proper 4

1 Kings 18:20–21 (*or* 20–29), 30–39 *or* 1 Kings 8:22–23, 41–43
Psalm 96
Galatians 1:1–12
Luke 7:1–10

WE begin today a selection of passages from Galatians, possibly Paul's earliest letter, and we pick up again the consecutive reading of Luke's Gospel. 1 Kings 8:41–43 reminds us that, even in Old Testament times, God was concerned for all peoples on earth – something beautifully celebrated in today's Psalm; while the story of Elijah in 1 Kings 18 raises vividly the question of the nature of faith. Both these themes are taken up in the New Testament readings.

Galatians is probably addressed to the Gentile congregations founded on Paul's first missionary journey, recorded in Acts 13–14. If so, they are his first missionary babies! He cares for them passionately, fiercely denouncing those who are disturbing them and trying to distort the gospel of Christ. We discover the problem later: some Jewish Christian missionaries had followed Paul to these churches, and tried to persuade them to accept circumcision as Jews. Verse 10 probably reflects their accusation of Paul – that he was toning down the demands of the gospel in order to 'please' the Galatians.

We will trace Paul's arguments against them in the coming weeks. Here at the start, like Elijah on Mount Carmel, he simply faces them with his claim – that *his* gospel is the true one, directly revealed by God. The first and last verses of the passage refer to his vision of Christ on the Damascus Road (Acts 9).

The Gospel reading points us toward one of the arguments Paul will develop in Galatians. Jesus' words about the centurion are truly remarkable: although a Gentile, he has greater faith than any Jew Jesus has met. Luke does not spell out how this can be, but later he introduces us to another centurion, Cornelius (Acts 10), who likewise exercises faith in Jesus, and then dramatically receives the Holy Spirit, without being circumcised as a Jew – thus showing that now God shows no partiality (Acts 10:34). God has broken down the age-long distinction between Jews and Gentiles and accepts all only on the basis of faith, and not because of adherence to any nationality, religion or law.

But all that is in the future. Here Luke prepares the way by enabling us to see some of the universal features of faith illustrated by this centurion. First, faith focuses upon Christ rather than on human need. Though deeply concerned about his servant, the centurion is moved primarily by his remarkable awareness of Jesus' in-built authority. Second, faith forces a new assessment of the self. The elders call him worthy, and doubtless he was, but he measures himself differently: 'I did not judge myself worthy to come to you.' The standard of measurement is Jesus, not social approval. Third, faith responds to Jesus' word. Luke places this story straight after the 'Sermon on the Plain' (6:20–49). So when the centurion says, 'Only speak the word ...', we realize that he cannot have this word without also having all Jesus' other words as well – as indeed Jesus himself makes clear, for he makes preaching the gospel and healing a single, two-pronged ministry (see Luke 4:18). This is the faith which Jesus calls 'great'!

* * *

– Proper 5

1 Kings 17:8–16 (*or* 8–24)
Psalm 146 *or* 30
Galatians 1:11–24
Luke 7:11–17

TODAY'S readings gather around the themes of prophets and faith, and raise some fascinating and challenging questions for today.

Elijah lives by obedience to the word of God, and the widow of Zarephath learns to do this too, even through great pain. When she sees her son alive again, she accepts that Elijah is a true prophet: 'Now I know that you are a man of God, and that the word of the Lord in your mouth is truth.'

Something similar happens when Jesus also raises a widow's son from the dead. The crowd reacts by calling him a prophet – in fact, 'A great prophet has risen among us!' God has visited his people! Why do they draw this conclusion? The answer lies in their understanding of the word of God. A 'prophet' speaks the words of God, but God's words are understood in a particular way. They once called the world into being: 'And God said, let there be light, and there was light' (Genesis 1:3). Words are distinguished by their creative power, power even to raise the dead. When the crowd calls Jesus a great prophet, they are identifying him as the prophet promised by Moses in Deuteronomy 18:15: 'The Lord your God shall raise up for you a prophet like me from among your own people; you shall heed such a prophet!' So God's word as power cannot be separated from God's word as instruction, and the crowd realize they must listen to, and obey, this great prophet now revealed before them.

Authentic Christian faith, we learn, is marked by obedience to the words of God as spoken by Jesus Christ. It is essentially something practical rather than cerebral: a confession, followed by a reformation.

73

But prophets are not always proved by words of power in this way. In the Galatians passage Paul claims strongly to be a prophet: his description of his call is deliberately comparable to Jeremiah's (Jeremiah 1:5). He insists on it, because opponents were suggesting that his gospel was his own invention, in independence of the truly authoritative Jerusalem apostles. 'Oh no!' Paul replies. 'I did not have much contact with Jerusalem, it is true, but I did not avoid them. I did not go, because I did not need to; God had revealed his Son to me without intermediary.'

The interesting thing is that Paul does not appeal to any words of power he had uttered to prove his prophetic status. He had performed some miracles in the Galatian churches, according to Acts (14:3), and he refers to these later (Galatians 3:5). But he does not mention them here. Why not?

The answer is because true faith never rests on proof. The widow of Zarephath had to trust that Elijah was a true prophet before ever her son was restored to life – see the story of how she made a snack for him! The widow of Nain and the pall-bearers did not resist Jesus' approach, but willingly stopped the funeral procession for him. Faith receives its confirmation after the point of no return, and not before. Words of power from God are heard with the ears of faith.

* * *

– Proper 6

1 Kings 21:1–10 (or 1–14), 15–21a or 2 Samuel 11:26 – 12:10, 13–15
Psalm 5:1–8 or Psalm 32
Galatians 2:15–21
Luke 7:36 – 8:34

TODAY'S readings bring vividly before us the extravagant forgiveness and grace of God. The playground cry, 'That's not fair!' turns into a principle of justice that governs human relationships in all civilized societies. We expect to be treated justly by the law, and by our fellow human beings. So it can be difficult to take on board the realization that unfairness is at the heart of the Christian gospel.

But of course Paul does not call it that. He calls it 'justification by faith', and this Galatians passage is a most important summary-statement of his teaching about this. The point is this: God does not measure us against a list of rules, so as to decide whether or not we qualify for heaven. The result of this would be disastrous: 'No one will be justified by the works of the Law' (Galatians 2:16b). So God refuses to give us what we deserve, and, against justice, justifies us through Christ.

David experiences this dramatically in Nathan's amazing assurance, 'The Lord has taken away your sin' (2 Samuel 12:13). Justice would demand the penalty for a murderer, but David is spared. The sinful woman in the Gospel passage should receive the straight rebuke which Simon the Pharisee clearly has in mind, but instead she experiences love, acceptance and forgiveness from Jesus and comes away feeling, no doubt, that Jesus prizes her more than Simon his host, because of his words in verses 44–47. Such forgiveness and acceptance are celebrated in Psalm 32: 'Blessed are those whose sin the Lord does not count against them' (v. 2).

The condition of such acceptance is simply confession. David could have blustered with Nathan, and continued the cover-up. But instead he came clean, 'I have sinned against the Lord.' The woman was ready publicly to renounce her sinful life-style, and to risk public shame in order to get to Jesus. The Psalmist reminds himself of the agony when he tried to keep silent about his sin (v. 3). As soon as he acknowledged it, forgiveness was immediately there.

Paul looks at it from a challenging angle in Galatians 2. If God simply justifies us like this, then religion can actually be a hindrance, rather than a help. He had given up his Judaism, with its emphasis on scrupulous observance of life-style rules, festivals and prayer-times, because he realized that it was incompatible with faith. This seems extraordinary. But he knew that, in the long run, religion alone has nothing to offer social outcasts like the woman of Luke 7. And indeed he had discovered – horror of horrors – that his religion had actually led him to persecute God's Messiah. So when Peter tried to reintegrate religion into Christian faith, Paul was horrified again and opposed the great apostle publicly (Galatians 2:11–14).

Religious observance can cushion us against a realistic encounter with God, with our eyes open to our sinfulness before him. Simon the Pharisee warns us. Let us hear the warning!

★ ★ ★

– Proper 7

1 Kings 19:1–4 (or 1–7), 8–15a or Isaiah 65:1–9
Psalms 42–43 or Psalm 22:19–28
Galatians 3:23–29
Luke 8:26–39

TODAY'S readings are designed to give hope to the hopeless. The Gospel passage introduces us to a complete no-hoper, a poor man whose mind is so deranged that he lives naked among the tombs, isolated from all normal human contact. We can only imagine the pain and the slow loss of hope felt by his friends and relatives, as for a long time they had tried to rescue him in vain. He symbolizes for us all such people: so victimized by powers within them – physical, emotional, mental or even demonic – that they are condemned to a half-life, confined within the tight horizons of their incapacity.

Out of the boat steps Jesus, and with him a power which by a word is able to restore this poor man. It doesn't often happen like that, but Christians believe in a Saviour who can deliver such people and who anyway draws close, unlike those who abandoned this man to the uncleanliness of the graveyard. This hope has sustained many a carer through long days and nights of selfless labour.

76

The Psalms (42 and 43 – clearly originally one Psalm) introduce us to the heart of such an experience. The writer is crippled by depression. He remembers the time when he was filled with joy in worship (42:4), but it seems like another world. Now he has been washed away by a torrent (42:7). But even in his depression he reaches out in hope to God, for he knows that his condition is abnormal, and that God who is a rock (42:9) and stronghold (43:2) will one day restore his capacity for joy and delight (43:4). Even within deep depression, hope is possible, for it rests on translating sorrow into longing for something better (42:1–2).

In the case of Elijah we see another such experience. In his case the depression is reactive: he has just had an amazing spiritual high on Mount Carmel, where he has seen the power of God at work in an amazing way. Suddenly – probably because of tiredness – his feelings collapse, he cannot cope with another challenge, and he ends up alone and suicidal in the desert. But God steps in with a hidden sustenance and takes him away for a rest-cure on Mount Horeb. It takes time, but eventually he is back again.

Paul reminds us that, by nature, we are all prisoners, held prisoners by the Law because of our incapacity to obey this statement of God's will. God's Law, he says elsewhere, is 'holy, righteous and good' (Romans 7:12), and condemns all who are less than that. But there is hope for those who simply reach out in faith, like the demoniac on the beach whose very ravings were a prayer for deliverance, and like the Psalmist and Elijah, who cast themselves on God in their dejection. Such faith by itself, says Paul, turns slaves into heirs and heiresses liable to inherit Abraham's fortune through Christ (Galatians 3:29).

None of the greatest sinners, nor any of the most complete no-hopers, are beyond the capacity of God to touch and heal.

* * *

77

– Proper 8

2 Kings 2:1–2, 6–14 *or* 1 Kings 19:15–16, 19–21
Psalm 77:1–2, 11–20 *or* Psalm 16
Galatians 5:1, 13–25
Luke 9:51–62

THE Epistle reading from Galatians 5 unpacks the meaning of Christian freedom by contrasting the works of the flesh (vv. 19–21) with the fruit of the Spirit (v. 22). Paul knew that it was just as possible for Christian people as for anyone else to bite and devour each other (v. 15) by indulging in hatred, discord, jealousy, fits of rage, selfish ambition, dissentions, factions and envy (v. 20) – such a beautiful collection of regular human foibles! But the Gospel reading reveals how the nicest people can become trapped by history into an ossified relation of official hostility out of which they cannot break. The Samaritans refuse hospitality to Jesus and his disciples, and then in righteous indignation James and John propose an appropriately hostile response. Out of the highest religious motives, the works of the flesh are given full rein. How do you escape from them? It takes the radical action of Jesus, who simply passes through quietly, absorbs the hatred and accepts the homelessness. He thus displays at least five segments of the fruit of the Spirit!

In the sayings which follow, Jesus turns the incident into a pattern of discipleship. Behind 'the works of the flesh' lies the desire to possess, to be recognized as right, to have status and power. The disciples of Jesus must lay aside all this, and be ready to accept homelessness with their Lord. Jesus demands of us a loyalty greater than that to our closest and dearest relatives.

Does he mean this literally? Elsewhere he criticizes people strongly for evading their responsibility to their parents, contained in the fourth Commandment (Mark 7:9–13). Sayings like this are known as focal instances – that is, Jesus' radical demand on us, his disciples, is focused by showing what it could mean; following him is more important even than having a home and caring for elderly parents. Of course, he may permit us to have possessions and command us to care for elderly parents but this central demand overrides all else: go and proclaim the Kingdom of God! (v. 60), in and through all you do.

The parallel with the story of the call of Elisha in the Old Testament reading (1 Kings 19:19–21) brings out the significance of proclaiming the Kingdom of God. Just as Elisha appointed Elisha to succeed him as prophet, so Jesus appoints his followers to a prophetic ministry before the world: 'proclaim the Kingdom!' Elisha instinctively knew what this meant. Without hesitation, he sacrificed his most prized possession – the twelve yoke of oxen, for which doubtless he was a local celebrity.

The fruit of the Spirit can be very costly to produce. The tree needs to be well manured by burying under it all those possessions, ambitions and desires which might otherwise produce very different works. Those who belong to the Christ, Paul tells us, have crucified the flesh with its passions and desires (Galatians 5:24).

Today's readings challenge us to careful prayer and thought about the level and quality of our discipleship.

*   *   *

– Proper 9

2 Kings 5:1–14 *or* Isaiah 66:10–14
Psalm 30 *or* Psalm 66:1–9
Galatians 6:7–16 (*or* 1–16)
Luke 10:1–11, 16–20

The theme of mission links today's readings. The seventy-two disciples were thrown into the deep end by Jesus, no doubt feeling like lambs among wolves (Luke 10:3) as they went out without even basic equipment for travelling. The point was to make them walking advertisements for the truth they were proclaiming: the presence of the kingdom. If God could heal the sick through their hands, then he would surely protect and provide for them. Giving

79

hospitality to these messengers, therefore, meant becoming part of their mission and entering the peace which they brought from God (v. 7).

Not all mission will be carried on like this, but the principle of the walking advertisement is essential. We see this in Paul. He adopted the opposite pattern, in fact: he refused to accept hospitality from the people he travelled to, and insisted on supporting himself. But the reason he gave made this an advertisement, also: the gospel was Good News, and he wanted to preach it free of charge (1 Corinthians 9:14–18).

Not everyone will be called to travelling mission like this. But we can all look outwards, says Paul in the Epistle reading: 'While we have opportunity, let us do good to all, particularly to those who belong to the household of faith' (v. 10). He warns the Galatians against a bad way of doing mission, exemplified in his opponents, who had been trying to persuade the Galatians to be circumcised: 'They want you to be circumcised, so that they may boast in your flesh!' (v. 13). Scalp-hunting is a very bad motivation for mission. But Paul himself shows a different way. So in love with Jesus Christ, and so aware of the new creation which he has experienced through Christ that he cannot keep silent about the cross, he must boast about it (vv. 14–15). He speaks the peace of the missionary on all who will live by this rule (v. 16).

For many of us, opportunities are as limited as they were for the little Israelite slave-girl who served Naaman's wife. How much does a slave-girl count in the affairs of the nations? But she knew what she knew and did not keep silent, because she loved the people she served, even though they had wrenched her away from her own family and country. 'If only my master would see the prophet who is in Samaria! He would cure him of his leprosy' (v. 3). Her integrity and genuineness shone so brightly that the great commander believed her and set off, willing to spend a fortune. She was a walking advertisement.

We can start by reaching out to each other, bearing one another's burdens, to 'fulfil the law of Christ' (Galatians 6:2). But when we have learned to do that, there is a world of need waiting to feel our touch as we reach out in the name of Christ, whose cross can bring hope in darkness. The world still needs such walking advertisements of his faith and love.

* * *

– Proper 10

Amos 7:7–17 *or* Deuteronomy 30:9–14
Psalm 82 *or* Psalm 25:1–10
Colossians 1:1–14
Luke 10:25–37

THIS Sunday sees the beginning of a series of readings from Colossians, alongside the continuing series from Luke. In these powerful opening verses, Paul first gives thanks for the Colossians' faith (vv. 3–8), and then prays for them (vv. 9–14). In both cases the report of his prayer expands into comments, in the first case about the spread of the gospel (vv. 6–8), and in the second case about the reasons for thanksgiving (vv. 12–14).

What does this glorious passage have in common with the parable of the Good Samaritan, today's Gospel reading? The connection emerges when we reflect on the way in which Paul's prayer is full of Old Testament and Jewish language and ideas. He uses the language of Israel as he gives thanks for their faith, their love for all the saints, and their hope focused on heaven. He uses the language as he prays that they may know God's will, please him in every good work and give thanks to the Father who has given them an inheritance and brought them into his kingdom by redemption and forgiveness of sin.

The Colossian believers were probably mainly Gentiles, and here is Paul praying that they may fully enjoy the relationship with God which Israel was supposed to have. On what basis does Paul transfer this relationship to Gentiles? This is a long and complicated story which takes us to the heart of Paul's theology, but we see the way being paved by passages like the parable of the Good Samaritan.

Contrary to popular belief, the parable does not simply mean, 'Do good to your neighbour'. It also says more than, 'Do your best to show compassion across barriers of racial hostility, like that between Jews and Samaritans'. The point is that it is the impure Samaritan sinner who fulfils the will and love of God, while the priest and Levite fail to do so, precisely because of their deep passion for God. They avoid the wounded man, not because they do not care, but because they will be disqualified from their Temple duties if they handle a corpse. So their desire for purity leads them into disobedience, while the Samaritan's disregard of such issues enables him to obey the first command of the Law (Deuteronomy 6:5), recited morning and evening by every Jew.

The parable of the Good Samaritan thus paves the way for the worldwide gospel in which Paul rejoices (Colossians 1:6). The vital thing is the orientation of the heart towards God. If the heart is right, then detailed regulations become unimportant – even things commanded in the Law. In fact, the Law says this too, as we see in the reading from Deuteronomy 30. 'God's word is not a distant prize, but very near you ... in your mouth and in your heart so that you may obey it.' When Paul quotes this passage in Romans 10:6–10, he makes it very clear that it is through Christ alone that the heart is re-created for obedience in this way. And this re-creation is now possible for *all* through the power of the Spirit – not just for Jews. Paul give thanks that he has actually seen it in the faith, hope and love now displayed by the Colossians.

* * *

– Proper 11

Amos 8:1–12 *or* Genesis 18:1–10a
Psalm 52 *or* Psalm 15
Colossians 1:15–28
Luke 10:38–42

THERE is an interesting balance between the Gospel reading and the story of Abraham and his visitors in Genesis 18. Martha is gently rebuked by Jesus for thinking that hospitality is more important that listening to his teaching. But, on the other hand, it was through being hospitable that Abraham got to hear God's word for him and Sarah. Ordinary things like cooking or working can either distract us and block the Spirit, or form a channel and opportunity for the Spirit. What makes the difference?

The difference appears when we ask what really grips and fires our imagination. Imagination creates longing, and fuels desire. It is fundamental to our make-up as human beings. C. S. Lewis called it joy, as he attempted to name that inarticulate yearning which sometimes wells up inside us.

Of course, it can be corrupt. Our imagination can be sparked in this way by bad objects and desires. In Psalm 52 we meet the man who plots destruction, who loves evil more than good, who above all trusted in abundant riches, and sought refuge in wealth. Similarly in the Amos passage we meet wheeler-dealers who cheat the poor by increasing the weights on their market scales, by adding dust to the wheat they sell, and by slightly reducing the size of the standard measure, the *ephah*. They long for festival days and sabbaths to end, so that they can get back to trading. Their imagination is gripped and drawn by money.

That is the way of disaster and ruin, Amos tells his hearers. In the long run, the capacity to receive anything better is destroyed; people will want to hear God, but they simply will not be able to. The picture in Amos 8:12 points to a society adrift, desperately seeking something beyond the merely material, but unable to find it.

This all helps us to understand Jesus' words to Martha. Hospitality is important of course, and Mary understood this as much as her sister. But Mary was consumed with such a desire to listen to Jesus that her sense of propriety as a hostess went out of the window! She could not tear herself away. She was gripped. For Martha, on the other hand, love for Jesus meant serving him a meal. Jesus gently tells her that feeding the spirit is more important than feeding the body.

That is the difference between Martha and Abraham. Abraham was the friend of God (Isaiah 41:8; James 2:23). The priority of his relationship with God was absolute. Martha's horizons were much smaller. For her, the ordinary blocked the Spirit. For him, it could not.

The size of our horizons will be measured by the reading from Colossians: a magnificent presentation of Jesus Christ (probably an early hymn, in fact) which appeals first and foremost to the imagination rather than the intellect. Intellect follows along behind, asking questions, but imagination or joy goes on ahead, prompting adoration of this Christ who is before all things, and in whom all things are reconciled to God. Do we long to know this Christ above all else?

* * *

– Proper 12

Hosea 1:2–10 *or* Genesis 18:20–32
Psalm 85 *or* Psalm 138
Colossians 2:6–15 (*or* 6–19)
Luke 11:1–13

TODAY'S readings present us, in different ways, with the challenge of engagement with the world. The temptation to withdraw into spiritual comfort has always been alluring, but the Fathers of the monastic tradition quickly realized that God was actually calling them to a different form of engagement,

84

not to withdrawal. We will see what this is as we reflect on these passages.

In Colossians the engagement is ideological – that is, it concerns ideas. Paul wants the church in Colossae to 'live in Christ ... rooted and built up in him and established in the faith, just as you were taught'. Paul knew that there were many philosophical and religious ideas in the air at Colossae; in fact, religious syncretism (combining ideas from different sources) was very common, and Paul knew that the gospel could easily be watered down with inputs from paganism or Judaism. He urges them to understand how God's fullness dwells in Christ, so that they need not incorporate bits of other religions into their faith. In today's pluralistic world, the gospel makes the same unique claim upon us.

In Hosea the engagement is much more personal and direct. God calls his prophet to marry a prostitute, so as to experience for himself the pain of rejection which God felt at the unfaithfulness of his people. This prophetic act spoke volumes to Hosea's contemporaries (whether they heard or not): God is as involved with his people as if he were married to them. Occasionally we hear talk about the prophetic role of the Church in today's society. If Hosea is our model, then we will not assume such a role until we are deeply involved, tasting its bitterness and sharing its pain – or, more precisely, God's pain – at the twistedness of people's lives.

Abraham too was a prophet. God revealed to him the coming destruction of Sodom, where Abraham's nephew Lot was living. So Abraham prays for the city, clearly with Lot especially in mind. But he does not pray that God will save Lot from the destruction, but that the city may be saved because of the presence of Lot and his family. This is why the prayer is so tentative: Abraham is asking God to change his mind.

What impudence! But actually Jesus encourages us to be impudent in prayer in the Gospel reading, like the man who impudently knocks up his neighbour late at night to ask for bread. The word translated 'persistence' in Luke 11:8 means more literally 'shamelessness' or 'impudence'. The point is that he wants the bread

85

for others, and to such prayer Jesus attaches the extravagant promise of verses 9–10. Why, you can even ask God for the Holy Spirit (v. 13) – an unthinkably impudent request for first century Jews! – and he will answer, if you ask so that you may serve others.

The ministry of prayer as an engagement with the needs of the world: the monastic tradition of the Church reminds us how vital this is. But we do not have to join a religious Order to take up this ministry. By the power of the Spirit, we can imitate the impudence of Abraham right now in pleading with God for this suffering and distracted world.

★   ★   ★

– Proper 13

Hosea 11:1–11 *or* Ecclesiastes 1:2, 12–14; 2:18–23
Psalm 107:1–9, 43 *or* Psalm 49:1–12
Colossians 3:1–11
Luke 12:13–21

L UKE's Gospel displays a special interest in issues of wealth and poverty. There are several warnings against the peril of riches, as in today's Gospel reading (see also Luke 1:53, 6:24f., 16:19–31, for example), and several places where voluntary poverty is commended (12:33, 18:24f., 19:8), or where the gospel message is made specially relevant to the poor (1:52f., 2:8ff., 4:18, 6:20f.). Today's passage has much to say to a materialistic age like ours, and sets a particular challenge before the Church: how may society around us see that we live by a different set of values, and not by the materialistic creed of our culture?

Luke's answer to this is very clear: those who truly believe that life does not consist in the abundance of possessions will express that faith by giving: 'Sell your possessions and give alms. Make purses for yourselves that do not wear out, an unfailing treasure in heaven … For where your treasure is, there your heart will be also'

(12:33f.). In a world of desperate need, our freedom from all kinds of greed (v. 15) will be signalled by our readiness to part with our possessions for the sake of others.

This is the cutting edge of Christian discipleship. Today's readings gather around this theme and show us the roots of this attitude towards possessions. First, the uselessness of wealth is the theme of the Ecclesiastes reading. The author has experienced all that money can buy (see also 2:8–11), and ends up calling at all vanity of vanities, because (a) it brings no true gain, (b) it causes much hard work, and (c) it must all be left behind. We need to share his down-to-earth perspective. Our reading should really include the last verses of chapter 2, where the author gives a positive response to the despair (2:20) he has just expressed: seeking joy is what life is all about, and God alone is the giver of true joy, to all who please him and seek wisdom.

Second, our accountability to God is the focus of the Gospel passage. 'This very night your soul is required of you!' There is someone – God – who has the right to require our souls, because ultimately we belong to him. Later in the passage Jesus expresses God's expectations: 'From everyone to whom much has been given, much will be required; and from the one to whom much has been entrusted, even more will be demanded' (12:48). We must render account to God for the way we have used resources which are ultimately his.

Third, our life elsewhere is the message of Colossians 3. The basis of the passage is 'You have died, and your life is hidden with Christ in God' (v. 3). We do not belong any more to this world, so we must live by our union with Christ, renouncing all kinds of wrong desire (v. 5), and all forms of wrong speech (v. 8), because our minds are set on 'things above', not on earthly things (v. 2).

These are the theological roots of a radical Christian attitude towards possessions. Our response demands careful thought and prayer.

– Proper 14

Isaiah 1:1, 10–20 *or* Genesis 15:1–6
Psalm 50:1–8, 22–23 *or* Psalm 33:12–22
Hebrews 11:1–3, 8–16
Luke 12:32–40

BELIEVING in the 'Second Coming' of Christ is something of a minority sport in today's Church. Various sects seem to have hijacked the belief and tainted it with fanaticism. And yet it is a venerable and vital expectation. Venerable, because it has always been part of Church doctrine; and vital, because the shape of biblical faith is essentially future-oriented. This future-orientation is the theme around which today's readings gather.

'I am your shield; your reward shall be very great,' the Lord says to Abraham (Genesis 15:1). For the author to the Hebrews, Abraham shows us what faith is all about, as he launches out in obedience to the promise of God, not seeing its fulfilment except with the eyes of faith. His nomadic life-style was only temporary, because God had promised him a dynasty and a home – a city, says Hebrews. Abraham never received it, because the reward is actually heavenly (Hebrews 11:16). So for this whole life he and his family were strangers and foreigners on the earth (v. 13), not at home because their home was elsewhere.

We are in the same position, says the author to the Hebrews. 'Faith is the assurance of things hoped for' (v. 1). That is, the essence of faith is basing action now on the conviction of a state of affairs yet to be. Faith is not just a state of mind, but involves a set of convictions about the destiny of the world, parallel to our convictions about the origin of the world. If we believe that the world has been created, then we may exercise the same faith and believe that it will one day be bettered by its Creator.

Psalm 33 expresses this faith. 'By the word of the Lord the heavens were made, and all their host by the breath of his mouth' (v. 6), and so, 'our soul waits for the Lord; he is our help and shield ...

Let your steadfast love ... be upon us, even as we hope in you'
(vv. 20, 22). Hope arises here out of convictions about origins.

In the New Testament, of course, this faith is focused upon Christ.
The Gospel reading expresses it vividly. We do not know when
the Son of Man may come, and so we must live like servants who
are always ready for their master's arrival. This does not mean just
a passive waiting, however; verses 32–34 describe the constant
scurrying-around of a church with this future-oriented faith.

The 'reward' is not something to be sought for itself, but the joyful
by-product of a faith directed at Christ himself. The servants focus
all their energy and anticipation on the master's return, only to be
invited to sit at his table when he comes. We can leave in the
realm of speculation the actual mechanics of the coming of
the Son of Man and the bettering of the world, but this future-
orientation is fundamental to Christian faith, and we dilute it at
great cost.

* * *

– Proper 15

Isaiah 5:1–7 *or* Jeremiah 23:23–29
Psalm 80:1–2, 8–19 *or* Psalm 82
Hebrews 11:29 – 12:2
Luke 12:49–56

TODAY'S Gospel reading contains some puzzles. What 'fire' has
Jesus come to bring (v. 49)? What is the 'baptism' which he is
eager to fulfil (v. 50)? Do these two pictures refer to the same
thing? And how are they related to the following description of
division in response to Jesus' ministry?

The reading from Jeremiah 23 suggests what fire may mean, for it
uses this image to refer to the word of God spoken in opposition
to the misleading words of the false prophets. So perhaps the 'fire'
Jesus brings is his prophetic message. But what then would be the
kindling for which he longs? Alternatively, 'fire' is a symbol of the

Holy Spirit, and Jesus could be looking forward with longing to the gift of the Spirit at Pentecost. But this would not fit well with the surrounding verses, especially the following words about division and conflict. Fire is also (not surprisingly) a regular symbol just for disaster of various kinds (see, for example, Revelation 8:5ff.), and maybe that is the simplest explanation of its meaning here.

But why should Jesus bring disaster on the earth? It depends on what sort of disaster is in mind. The picture of family conflict in verses 52–53 is drawn from Micah 7:5–6, where it expresses the alienation experienced by those who want to trust God in the midst of a society which has turned its back on him. Jesus tells his disciples that following him has a similar price-tag attached. The life of the servants who wait and work for their master to return will not be easy. The author to the Hebrews develops this thought in broader terms as he describes the faithfulness under fire of those who lived by faith in days past – as an example to us, who must also 'run with perseverance the race that is set before us'.

It has been a constant Jewish objection to Christian faith that Jesus announced the Kingdom, but the world was not redeemed. But we can see from a passage like this that Jesus apparently did not expect the world to be transformed by his ministry – far from it. A sense of the certain coming of final judgment runs through Luke chapter 12, but until that judgment arrives the earth will be afflicted with division symbolized by the persecution of his followers. In the puzzling verse 56, Jesus is probably referring to his own presence and ministry as a sign of that impending judgment. Like a cloud that heralds a storm, so he points to the final judgment for which all need to prepare.

He does not stand aloof from his suffering church. In all likelihood, the baptism in verse 50 is his coming death. He, too, was torn by the brokenness and hostility which afflicts our human race and indeed he longs to fulfil that role. What suffering lies ahead of us, as we follow him? Hebrews encourages us with the example of those who were carried through their pain by the vision of the one 'who, for the joy set before him, endured the cross, despising the shame, and is seated at the right hand of God'.

– Proper 16

Jeremiah 1:4–10 *with* Psalm 71:1–6 *or* Isaiah 58:9b–14 *with* Psalm
103:1–8
Hebrews 12:18–29
Luke 13:10–17

WE often speak of our choice of God. The Bible more often
speaks of God's choice of human beings; and a change of
emphasis in our testimonies might provide greater insight into the
workings of God in the human soul than any number of human
claims to have 'chosen' to become a Christian.

Jeremiah clearly did not want to be the prophet that God wanted
him to be. And we can hardly blame him. From the account in the
book that bears his name, his ministry was not popular: he had to
suffer rejection and ridicule, and his message was so unpopular that
he was thrown into prison at one stage. Small wonder, then, that
he objected, 'Ah, Lord God! Truly I do not know how to speak,
for I am only a boy.' Any excuse would seem sensible to avoid
such a appalling vocation. Jeremiah might well pray, with the
Psalmist, for refuge from such a ministry: 'In you, O Lord, I take
refuge; let me never be put to shame. In your righteousness deliver
me and rescue me; incline your ear to me and save me' – save me
from the calling you have given to me!

Jeremiah prophesied in Jerusalem at the time of the city's conquest
in 587 BCE. He went to Egypt with some of those who were not
taken captive to Babylon. He therefore lived in the context of
great national upheaval, and part of his message was to insist that
what was happening to God's city was the result of God's judgment. So Jeremiah's knowledge of God was not very different
from that of the writer of the Epistle to the Hebrews, who wrote
that God 'is a consuming fire'. He had no alternative but to hear
and obey, for this God is not one to be argued with.

Strangely enough, however, it is precisely this fearsome God of
Jeremiah who is the one who brings wholeness to broken lives.
The Gospel story reminds us that God is against that which

enslaves, and he is for that which heals those who are bowed low with pain and grief. He is against those who say that all is well when it is not; he is against those who use power, not to alleviate anguish, but to exploit their good fortune and ignore the cries of those who suffer. The 'entire crowd' cheered him on – Luke tends to portray Jesus as popular with ordinary people; there is no crowd to condemn him at the end, only the religious leaders. So we note and give thanks for the single-mindedness of Jesus in his compassion and his action, since his love never changes. And we stick with the vocation to follow him; where else can we go, since he alone has the words of life?

* * *

– Proper 17

Jeremiah 2:4–13 *with* Psalm 81:1, 10–16 *or* Sirach 10:12–18 *or*
Proverbs 25:6–7 *with* Psalm 112
Hebrews 13:1–8, 15–16
Luke 14:1, 7–14

JEREMIAH'S complaint against the people of Judah is that they have abandoned their God, only to put in his place nothing of significance. The oracle he speaks has the tone of a forsaken lover who is bewildered at the folly of the one who has left love and security in exchange for uncertainty, fear and disappointment. The prophet sees the generation of Israelites who were led out of Egypt through the wilderness as being less foolish, for when they received the Law through Moses at Sinai they were glad to be in a covenant relationship with God. Now the folly of the present generation has cut them off from his promises and his presence, and all they can hope for is desolation and defeat. The Psalmist takes up the theme of the people's faithlessness: 'O that my people would listen to me ... then I would quickly subdue their enemies ... I would feed you with the finest of the wheat, and with honey from the rock I would satisfy you.' Their faithless behaviour is inexplicable, since it will surely end in disaster.

The other readings are also concerned, in their way, with rational behaviour. Why should we act morally? Because of the promise of some repayment, or because virtue is its own reward? In the case of the Letter to the Hebrews, reasons are given for the kind of behaviour recommended – the reference to 'entertaining angels unawares' is probably an allusion to Abraham and Sarah's hospitality to the travellers in Genesis 18; three messengers from God visited them to tell them Sarah would have a son the following year.

The Gospel's exhortation to humility and generosity is made on the basis of the rewards which will be available in the kingdom of God. Here the issue becomes rather more value-laden than a simple discussion of motivation. The kingdom of God confronts all who are concerned with doing the will of God with the question of right behaviour for the sake of the behaviour itself. Elsewhere, we are commanded to do what is required of us, not for the sake of reward, but for the sake of the good itself. For Christian people, the discussion is taken to a different plane of discourse, for to believe that God rewards those who obey him is not the same as believing that we keep an eye on what best serves our interests. First, because in Jesus Christ God calls us to live in such a way that the interests of our neighbour are served rather than our own; and second because God is not just one more reward alongside others.

God holds out for us a set of values that are not located in a superficial kind of contract, in which we 'get what we pay for'. The reward of good behaviour for those who seek the mind of God is the knowledge that God delights in love and compassion, and that to behave in such way is to imitate him whose life and grace we are called to share. This is behaviour that is rooted in an understanding of life in the Spirit.

*   *   *

– Proper 18

Jeremiah 18:1–11 *with* Psalm 139:1–6, 13–18 *or* Deuteronomy
30:15–20 *with* Psalm 1
Philemon 1–21
Luke 14:25–33

MOST readers of this commentary will have visited a pottery at some time in their lives. The story of Jeremiah continues with his arresting metaphor of the potter's wheel. God is portrayed in it as one who creates as a potter creates a vessel, and who brings things to nothing just as the potter is able to reduce a jar-in-the-making back to a shapeless lump. This is a chilling picture of God for us who live in an age when we are aware of the importance of political choices in the world of international affairs. Aren't our freedoms curtailed by such a reading of the purposes of God?

And what about that Psalm? Isn't it quite alarming to think of someone who knows 'when I sit down and when I rise up', who 'discerns my thoughts from far away'? And do we want to have someone around to whom it can be said, 'Even before a word is on my tongue, O Lord, you know it completely'? Indeed, such an image might well 'hem me in, behind and before', in a sense much more oppressive than the Psalmist intends. Where is our freedom? we may want to ask.

The answer is that it is guaranteed when God is known as the Father of Jesus Christ, because, in Christ, humanity is called to share in the life of God. This God is not one who oppresses, but one who generates creativity and who loves the kind of intimacy which makes for growth and the development of all human potential.

Such a God is set over against any kind of devotion which diminishes the image of God in us all. That is why the choices are so stark which confront the people of Israel in Deuteronomy. They have witnessed God's presence and provision over the years. Will they now acknowledge his claim to be their God for ever, or will they go after that which is less than God? Will they choose right or wrong, life or death? These choices may seem oversimplified – certainly it is not always easy to discern in the choices we have to make which is the way of life. But the choice set before the Israelites in this story is one of fundamental attitudes, perceptions and direction; which way do you want your life to go? Answering this question is sometimes easier than is living up to its implications.

The choice St Paul set before Philemon was simply concerned with a small favour. Onesimus, a slave whose name means 'useful', had evidently run away from Philemon's household and somehow or other came into contact with the apostle, who had found him very 'useful' to himself. Having made use of his services, Paul sends him back to Philemon, certainly with the certainty that Onesimus should not be punished for running away. It is possible that the hidden message, the broad hint, is that Paul wants him sent back to him as a gift, so that he can continue his 'useful' service. We do not know what Philemon decided. Later in the first century there was a bishop of Ephesus called Onesimus. It is comforting to think that this might have been the former slave, given his freedom, who rose to lead the Christian community not so far away from Colossae. But we do not know.

What we do know is that the choices we make, no matter how small the issue, are all, without exception, the stuff of the kingdom of God.

★   ★   ★

95

– Proper 19

Jeremiah 4:11–12, 22–28 *with* Psalm 14 *or* Exodus 32:7–14 *with*
Psalm 51:1–10
1 Timothy 1:12–17
Luke 15:1–10

THE prophecy of Jeremiah is concerned here with the judgment that is to come upon the inhabitants of Jerusalem
for their apostasy. 'A hot wind' will scorch the earth and all
that is in it, and we need to remember that 'wind' is the same
word in Hebrew as 'Spirit'. This is God coming in judgment
upon his people. The reason for their condemnation was
that they had behaved as if God were not to be reckoned with, like
the fools in Psalm 14 who had said that there is no God. The
Psalmist continues, 'They are corrupt, they do abominable
deeds; there is no one who does good.' The evil deeds of the
people of Judah stemmed from their forgetting their covenant
with God.

This is not the same as saying that absence of belief in God
necessarily leads to immoral behaviour – we probably all know of
atheists who are deeply moral, and we know that the profession of
Christian faith is no guarantee that we shall act morally; indeed, we
are aware of moral philosophers who say that Christian morality is
insufficiently good. For the Psalmist, the issue was more clear-cut;
those who did wrong denied God. Hence the cry, 'O that
deliverance for Israel would come from Zion! When the Lord
restores the fortunes of his people, Jacob will rejoice; Israel will be
glad.' Here is a cry borne of the experience of absence from God,
of exile from him.

The 'Pastoral Epistles' – those to Timothy and Titus – are now
generally reckoned to have been written by someone other than
Paul himself. He wrote in Paul's name in order to carry on the
tradition of his preaching and teaching, to honour his memory
and to continue his ministry. This is not a question of falsehood
or trickery, but an instance of loyalty to a tradition. The writer
celebrates Paul's memory; his calling is remembered, and he is

depicted as the archetypal apostle, changed from blasphemer and persecutor to devoted follower and proclaimer of the good news of Jesus. The grace of God shown to Paul is the subject also of the Gospel reading, where we see that the repentance of the individual person is a matter of concern to God. The Greek word for repentance means a change of mind, and that involves adjusting our mental set to the values of the kingdom of God.

Moses might provide an example of that. On Mount Sinai he enjoyed the closest possible relationship with God, and was given the Ten Commandments. Yet even while he was there, the people of Israel were deserting the God who had led them out of slavery in Egypt and were constructing a golden calf to worship. Moses, the man of God who was passionately concerned for the good of the people, prayed to God on their behalf and persuaded him not to destroy the people but to make a great nation from Moses's descendants only. Here was a man who knew God, and who was prepared to forfeit his own spiritual well-being for the sake of those committed to his charge. We often hear of the exploits of those who are prepared to give their lives for the sake of others; how many of us are prepared to sacrifice our salvation?

* * *

– Proper 20

Jeremiah 8:18 – 9:1 *with* Psalm 79:1–9 *or* Amos 8:4–7 *with* Psalm 113
1 Timothy 2:1–7
Luke 16:1–13

> *There is a balm in Gilead / To make the wounded whole;*
> *There is a balm in Gilead / To heal a sin-sick soul.*
> *Sometimes I feel discouraged / And think my work's in vain;*
> *But then the Holy Spirit / Revives my soul again.*
> *There is a balm in Gilead / To make the wounded whole;*
> *There is a balm in Gilead / To heal a sin-sick soul.*

TODAY'S passage from Jeremiah has the prophet lamenting the desolation of Jerusalem after it has been laid waste by its enemies. The prophet bewails God's absence and calls for help now that the city has been laid waste: is there really no help; 'is there no balm in Gilead?'

The old spiritual suggested that there was comfort, but here there is no balm; the question is desperate. 'My joy is gone, grief is upon me, my heart is sick,' says the prophet. This is the kind of context in which the Psalmist might well ask, 'How long, O Lord? Will you be angry forever? Will your jealous wrath burn like fire?' The Psalmist wants God's anger to be shown to the nations who have destroyed the city: 'Pour out your anger on the nations that do not know you, and on the kingdoms that do not call on your name, for they have devoured Jacob and laid waste his habitation.' He writes for an age later than Jeremiah, when the mood of the religious thinkers was that God had punished his people enough, and that the surrounding nations had profited too much from Judah's and Israel's defeat. Now the cry is that they be punished for their pride. But earlier, it was God's own people who deserved judgment.

The contrast of this desire for vengeance with the desire in 1 Timothy for prayer on behalf of rulers is quite marked. For a number of reasons it is unlikely that St Paul himself wrote these 'Pastoral Epistles' that bear his name; what is reflected here is a situation in which the Church, presumably before it has known any great persecution on the part of the state, is able to believe that political leaders are there 'so that we may lead a quiet and peaceable life in all godliness and dignity'. A peaceable political state could provide the context in which the gospel could be preached. There are dangers in this view, of course, for the preaching of the gospel may result in conflict with the state's values, as the early Church was soon to discover.

The 'manager' in the Gospel passage can stand for leaders in any context who do not act in charity and compassion towards those who are set under them. Forgiveness, as an instrument of policy, has been shown in many cases to be an effective way of building community and enabling people and groups to function, but it must be exercised equitably; the problem is, all too often, that those at the top of the pile expect to be forgiven, only to exploit their position over their juniors. If we were to read this parable as an allegory (as, it must be admitted, many commentators have done) then we might observe that God is the one who forgives unconditionally, and expects those who are forgiven also, in their turn, to forgive. The allegorical interpretation does not alter the practical, ethical message; it simply gives it both more force and a theological grounding.

*　*　*

– Proper 21

Jeremiah 32:1–3a, 6–15 *with* Psalm 91:1–6, 14–16
or Amos 6:1a, 4–7 *with* Psalm 146
1 Timothy 6:6–19
Luke 16:19–31

AT the very moment of imminent defeat, Jeremiah tells King Zedekiah of God's purpose to restore the future fortunes of Judah. He tells of his purchase of a field which he or his descendants will claim, once the nation has been brought back from exile in Babylon. The story is told as a reminder of the faithfulness of God, even when he has given the city of Jerusalem over to foreign invaders as a punishment for Judah's departure from the covenant. There may be no hope for the present, but the future is in the hand of God. It is this kind of protection which the Psalmist can celebrate; not that God will preserve his people from the implications and consequences of their actions, but that they may be certain of his continuing compassion and promises for them in the unknown future. 'Those who love me, I will deliver; I will protect those who know my name. When they call to me, I will answer them; I will be with them in trouble, I will rescue them and honour them.'

Amos is railing against the evils of God's people, who constantly refuse to listen to his warnings. Psalm 146 echoes the refrain, 'Do

not put your trust in princes, in mortals, in whom there is no help.'
It might not prove as simple for us as the scriptures seem to say that
it was for Jeremiah and his contemporaries. Our trust in God has
normally to be expressed in and through the relationships we have
with other people, and those who claim to have a hot-line to the
will of the Almighty are rightly regarded with suspicion.
However, the principle remains: in a context where knowledge of
the mind of God was a matter of consulting prophets, what
counted was the people's obedience to what was disclosed.
Although our ways of knowing God are rooted in the conviction
that God is known in the everyday jostle of human relationships
and concerns, what counts for us is our commitment to doing
the will of God, once we have discerned what it might be. As
the writer of 1 Timothy says, 'there is great gain in godliness
combined with contentment.'

This principle is to be applied to the ever-present problem of
wealth. (Note: it is wealth, not poverty, that is the problem.) What
values are appropriate to the person – or the community – which
has more than it can manage or know what to do with? We see in
the parable of the rich man and Lazarus the complete folly of a life-
style and set of values that are dictated by the demands of caring for
our earthly possessions. It is not so much that the relationships will
be reversed in the life to come; it is that the assumption that wealth
is a sign of ultimate well-being is *already* sufficient proof of folly.
Certainly, it is good to have enough money to live on, but a
society that condemns so many to live in poverty is foolish, as well
as mean and spiritually bankrupt. The values of the kingdom of
God demand more equal sharing of the good things of the world.
The values which God proposes for human society are applicable
immediately.

★　　★　　★

– Proper 22

Lamentations 1:1–6 *with* Lamentations 3:19–26 *or* Psalm 137
or Habakkuk 1:1–4; 2:1–4 *with* Psalm 37:1–9
2 Timothy 1:1–14
Luke 17:5–10

THE Book of Lamentations is traditionally ascribed to Jeremiah, but it is unlikely that he was the author. Although it dates from soon after the destruction of Jerusalem in 587 BCE, it could have been written in the twentieth century. Its bleak description of the city of Jerusalem after it was sacked by the Babylonians reads like something from a battlefield in Flanders or a modern bombed city. Jerusalem has been denuded of its people; all the brightness of city life is no more and there is nothing left, either of its commerce or of its fun. Yet the writer is still confident of God's compassion; his mercies are 'new every morning'.

In a similar way, the well-known lament in Psalm 137 for the bereft city expresses the Psalmist's sorrow at the sacking of Jerusalem. The writer pledges eternal fidelity to the memory of Jerusalem, even though its glory is now departed. How can the vicious sentiments in the final verse have a place in holy scripture? Because holy scripture not only contains the word of God addressed to humanity, but also the archetypal word which humanity addresses to God; one can imagine this curse on the lips of someone who saw such things happen to the little children of Jerusalem.

The prophet Habakkuk sets a slightly different tone – though not greatly so. Why is it that there is such evil, and why do the just have to suffer so? How terrible it is when 'the law becomes slack and justice never prevails'. Yet the prophets remain true to their calling. They write what they are called to write and speak what they are called to speak. The message is that those who are righteous will gain life by continuing to live in faithfulness to God. This text (Habakkuk 2:4) is the one made famous by St Paul's use of it to mean 'the one who by faith is righteous shall live'; here, in its original context, it calls for fidelity to the covenant, and patience for the working of God. The message of Psalm 37 is similar; do not 'fret' over evildoers – their end will come, and virtue is its own reward.

The two sections of the Gospel passage seem to be connected only by the catchword principle which focuses on the concept of obedience. To the person with faith, trees are obedient when told to plant themselves in the sea. This idea moves on to a consideration of the obedience that is required in servants. When the slave comes in from the field, his work is not done until he has finished serving his owner's desires.

It is possible that there is no connection intended between the opening statement and the continuing story. If they are to be taken together, then whatever the origin of these sayings in the tradition before they were written down, their juxtaposition here suggests that everything is at the disposal of those who have faith; they are privileged to exercise lordship over creation and they may expect obedience. Such is the reversal of the world's values that is to take place at the end of time, when the kingdom of God dawns.

* * *

– Proper 23

Jeremiah 29:1, 4–7 *with* Psalm 66:1–12
or 2 Kings 5:1–3, 7–15c *with* Psalm 111
2 Timothy 2:8–15
Luke 17:11–19

Now in captivity, the people are advised by Jeremiah to stay there. They are to settle, to marry, to buy land; indeed, they are to reckon with the fact that they must live there for the foreseeable future. Above all, they are to seek the well-being of the place to which they have been taken, for in its prosperity lies their own. The Psalm associated with this reading suggests praise to God for all his decisions about what happens to people; in the context

of the Jeremiah passage, it suggests that, whatever happens –
whether in the details or in the momentous events of life – God
remains God, worthy to be praised for his judgments, which will
turn out to be gracious, and his action, which puts his judgments
into effect.

The story of Naaman the leper is well known as an incident in the
life of the prophet Elisha. Of the points to be noted one might
mention the fame of the prophet, the pride of the Syrian
commander, the anxiety of the king, the good sense of the serving
maid, the willingness of Naaman to swallow his pride – and any
number of other details. What is most important, however, is the
discovery on the part of a non-Jew that 'there is no God in all the
earth except in Israel'. The Psalm is an appropriate ascription of
praise to God for his universal glory and care.

The Second Epistle to Timothy pictures Paul as the great preacher
of the gospel, suffering for his faithfulness, yet undiminished in his
enthusiasm. The writer (probably not Paul himself) reasserts the
gospel as he understands it, and urges that the tradition of teaching
must continue which started with the apostle. The emphasis on
'rightly explaining' is significant – it suggests the careful cutting of
'sections' of the truth, to enable people to take in what they need.
A sensitive approach to other people's learning is what is required.

The Gospel passage makes a connection with the story of Naaman,
the Syrian. It shows, first, the unity of those in need: no distinctions of race are made between the lepers who all need cleansing.
Neither does Jesus discriminate. What strikes him, though, is the
significant fact that it was the 'outsider' who alone returned to
express his thanks. This has implications for Luke's understanding
of the gospel; in the Acts of the Apostles this emphasis on its appeal
to those outside the traditional people of God will become
apparent. There are parallels for us, in a society in which many
wish to place barriers between people and make exclusions where
God invites all people to know and be known by him.

*   *   *

103

– Proper 24

Jeremiah 31:27–34 *with* Psalm 119:97–104
or Genesis 32:22–31 *with* Psalm 121
2 Timothy 3:14 – 4:5
Luke 18:1–8

THE lesson from Jeremiah is one of the most touching of Old Testament passages. Here the Lord God promises to restore a covenant relationship with the people, but which will be different than what existed prior to their exile. Formerly, God tells Jeremiah, the people had to apply themselves to keeping the covenant and knowing God. But when the nation's fortunes are restored, they will have no need of any exhortations to faithfulness, because God will give them his own Spirit, so they will keep his Law without any struggle.

The modern reader may wince at this prediction of automated obedience, but Christians will see it as a foretaste of life in the Holy Spirit, where what counts as good behaviour is not adherence to any set of standards or rules or law, but the expression of the Spirit of God (who is also the Spirit of the risen Jesus) in the loving life of the believer. The Psalmist celebrated the Law of God because it represented God's favour to Israel; it was thus a symbol of the covenant, as well as the content of it. It may stand as a metaphor, both for Christian adherence to the scriptures, and for the Christian's desire to do the will of God as the Spirit leads.

The lesson from Genesis tells the wonderful story of Jacob receiving his come-uppance at the hands of the angel of the Lord. He may have won the wrestling match, but he lived ever after with the wound received in the fight. His experience is not too dissimilar to life in the Spirit. We have no guarantee against harm; indeed, some of our ills arise because of our faith. And sometimes we limp a little, because we are called to 'bear in our body the marks of the Lord Jesus'. Faith is not the passport to a trouble-free existence; it is the awareness that whatever happens to us is shared by a God who loves us and who is with us in all of it.

The writer of 2 Timothy continues to exhort Timothy to exercise leadership in the Christian community by teaching the faith; his pastoral care is not separated from telling the people how to understand the scriptures in the light of Christ (in his case, the Jewish scriptures, whether in Hebrew or in Greek). Such an attachment to understanding the holy writings of the community is central to discipleship, and pastoral care which is held apart from Christian education is deficient.

Jesus' parable in Luke 8 is not the easiest to understand. Its basic message is relatively simple: there are those who will respond to requests on the basis of impatience and self-interest, but God delights in giving gifts to his people. Christian people therefore should pray without stopping, for to pray is to continue in conversation with God. Jesus' final sentence sounds like a weary sigh, emitted in the knowledge that, even though God is so gracious, men and women are inexplicably reluctant to talk and share their lives with him.

★   ★   ★

– Proper 25

Joel 2:23–32 *with* Psalm 65
or Sirach 35:12–17 *or* Jeremiah 14:7–10, 19–22 *with*
Psalm 84:1–7
2 Timothy 4:6–8, 16–18
Luke 18:9–14

THE prophet Joel looks forward with glad anticipation to the day, not just when the exiles will return to Jerusalem, but when the Lord himself will return and give his Spirit to the people, so that they will worship him in spirit and be marked out as his people. Then he will vindicate them for all that they have suffered at the hands of other nations. That is the picture that is also drawn in the Psalm which is associated with this reading: the people of God glad in their knowledge of him and giving thanks for his blessing, not only on themselves, but also on the earth itself.

The Wisdom of Jesus ben Sirach, otherwise known as Ecclesiasticus, is a typical example of Wisdom literature. Here the writer urges justice in human relationships, for God is no respecter of persons; when it says that he will not show partiality to the poor, it means that the possession or non-possession of wealth is not an issue when it comes to God's justice. What is important is whether the person has acted rightly; and both rich and poor are capable of good and evil. The Jeremiah passage returns again to the same theme of judgment and mercy which the lectionary has covered over the past few weeks. Here the prophet acknowledges the sins of the people before God, and prays for forgiveness. He is confident in God's abiding faithfulness, even if the tragedy facing Jerusalem is now unavoidable. Psalm 84 seems all the more poignant in such a context. The dwelling place of God is the Temple at Jerusalem, and those who once lived in God's house, ever singing his praise, were bereft of such blessings once the place has been desecrated and abandoned.

St Paul's memory is hallowed once again in 2 Timothy. The apostle is shown contemplating his end, reviewing his life and summing up his achievements. The writer has no doubt that Paul 'fought the good fight' and 'kept the faith'. He may have been beset by opposition throughout his ministry, and there is a tradition in the first Epistle of Clement that he was betrayed at the end by Christian opponents. But this hero of the faith is held up as the model disciple, whom all other disciples might emulate.

The parable of the Pharisee and the publican brings all the discussion about faith and faithfulness down to basics. What is significant is not so much the faithfulness of the disciple, but the faithfulness of God who is dependably gracious. In the sight of God, what is required is not the elaboration of our achievements, but the acknowledgement of our shortcomings. The grace of God is not out to minimize our successes, but to put into perspective our sometimes vaunted accomplishments. Paul himself knew (cf. Philippians 3) that everything he had done, for good or ill, counted nothing when set beside the infinite mercy of God. Today's readings invite us to a similar reflection upon the mercy we have all received.

Bible Sunday

Isaiah 45:22–25
Psalm 119:129–136
Romans 15:1–6
Luke 4:16–24

'BIBLE Sunday' presents an opportunity to celebrate the presence of the holy scriptures, not just in the life of the Church, but also in and among all humankind. Historically, it is certainly the Church within which the scriptures arose, but there is no doubt that their message is one for the whole of humankind, for they speak of God who became human in the person of Jesus.

The passage from Isaiah reminds us that the 'word' of God cannot easily be identified with a written text, for it existed and was active before anything was written. For Isaiah, that which God speaks is that which brings things into being, and it cannot fail to achieve what God wants it to create. 'From my mouth has gone forth in righteousness a word that shall not return' is indicative of Isaiah's understanding of the word of God, which calls all people to worship the one God, made known in Israel's history, and, for Christian people, known as the Father of Jesus Christ.

The Psalm reflects the wonder of the written Torah, or Law, of the Jewish nation as it is revered still. The Law is a sign of the covenant, and it is given to the Jewish nation as a mark of God's choice. In singing the praises of the Law, the Psalmist is also praising God for revealing it to the human race through the Jews. It is into this same inheritance that Christians enter, by the grace of God. St Paul catches the flavour of this when he writes to the Romans, 'For whatever was written in former days was written for our instruction, so that by steadfastness and by the encouragement of the scriptures we might have hope.' He refers, of course, to the Jewish scriptures, which formed the first Bible for the early Christians; the 'New' Testament, as we know it, was not finalized until later in Christian history.

From the very start, Christians have read the Jewish scriptures as though they speak of Christ. In a sense, of course, they do, though perhaps not in ways which Christians originally thought. Over the past two centuries, Christian scholars have come to recognize a little of the processes that went into the formation of the Christian Bible; it has become obvious that the primary meaning of Jewish scriptures is not simply as prophecy of Christ and the Church, but as integral to the life and faith of the Jewish people. To these were added, first, the letters of St Paul, along with other letters and the Gospels.

The story in Luke 4 is instructive; it shows how the earliest Christians used the text of the Bible to give meaning to their understanding of the significance of Jesus. But more than that, it shows, in a fashion typical of Jewish faith and continued among Christians, that texts are capable of many interpretations. The people who listened to Jesus in that synagogue would not have been surprised that he used the occasion to explore a novel meaning of the text; what they objected to was that he referred the text to himself. We, too, operate in this double way. The text of scripture has meaning in its context, the 'historical-grammatical sense', as Martin Luther called it; and from this has developed the biblical critical approach which is used throughout Western Christendom. But it also demands the understanding of faith, and so points to Jesus, as it were, in defiance not only of Jewish objections but also of any tradition which would limit the senses in which Jesus can be understood and known today and in any age.

* * *

Dedication Festival

1 Chronicles 29:6–12
Psalm 122
Ephesians 2:19–22
John 2:13–22

THERE is a dilemma at the heart of Christianity. It persists throughout the scriptures and concerns the value to be put on things physical – the handiwork both of God and of human beings. How far may places, trees and rocks be set apart and regarded as 'holy'? The answers vary along a spectrum. At one end there is superstition about 'things', an inability to move beyond seeing God in the present order (whether that be nature or some religious institution). At the other end is a refusal to see the sacred anywhere specific and to 'spiritualize' faith out of all engagement with the created order, lacking either ecological awareness or political cutting edge. The two poles emerge as equally limited. Both in their different ways short-circuit the essential integration between spirit and matter implied by belief in an incarnate God. Today's readings offer a warning to the contemporary Church as it tries to walk a fine line between thinly spread political activism on the one hand and navel-gazing 'spirituality' on the other. There are innumerable instances where we make a false distinction between our outer and our inner beings.

The Book of Chronicles, from which the first reading comes, endeavours to re-think long-held beliefs and adapt to a life-style no longer dependent on a king or on national freedom. Moving away from a traditional stress on prophecy, the small Jewish community under Persian rule is beginning to become a 'religion' and to emphasize the value of temple worship and ritual purity. In a time when alien rule seems likely to go on for ever and when no future messianic age is in view, the chronicler recommends political quietism, submission to destiny and a high view of religious practice – giving hope to Judah. The Lord is always with his people, especially when they are at worship.

The passage from Ephesians offers an interesting hinge between the positive view of religion, presented in the Old Testament reading, and the prophetic action of Jesus in the Gospel – implying judgment on the Jerusalem Temple. Ephesians emerges from a period, rather like that of Chronicles, in which the religious task is that of accommodating theology to political reality. The main difference is that there is no longer a sacrificial system or physical building upon which to focus. Instead, the author describes God's plan as being worked out on two different levels: the heavenly and the earthly. Here his images for the (earthly) Church will provide the basis for instruction in Christian behaviour. Jews and Gentiles are now members of one household, a building growing into a holy temple; but it is the Spirit, rather than a physical structure, which enables unity and growth. Despite the static imagery, there is some inner dynamism and movement within the secure, and conventional, scenario.

Temple imagery is used in a variety of ways in the New Testament. The Ephesians picture may be a development of Paul's 'Body of Christ' (1 Corinthians 12) taken with the tradition in John's Gospel that Jesus himself likened his own 'body' to the Temple. It is this second image which comes to the fore in the Gospel reading. Jesus makes his epiphany, or appearance, at the Temple in Jerusalem – and replaces the Temple as the place of God's revelation. Unlike the other Gospel accounts this happens at the very beginning of his ministry, and there is misunderstanding, typical of this Gospel, as to what he is really about. The notion of physical and spiritual realities as indivisible is expressed throughout the biblical material – not least in the person of Jesus. It points us towards the possibility of understanding the material world and human creativity – even our Church communities – as graced by God for mission. Where they remain static, as ends in themselves, they fall under judgment.

*   *   *

All Saints' Sunday

Daniel 7:1–3, 15–18
Psalm 149
Ephesians 1:11–23
Luke 6:20–31

THE visions of the Book of Daniel are remarkable creations, in which beasts of all kinds of awesome detail strike terror into the mind of the readers. The Book of Daniel was written to assert and encourage the faith of a community which, in the first part of the second century BCE, was under siege. The great encouragement here was that in the middle of all this terror, when God's people were suffering atrocious things for their faith, the image of 'one like a man' was set to remind them of the supreme value to God of those people, human beings, who comprised his saints: 'As for these four great beasts, four kings shall araise out of the earth. But the holy ones of the Most High shall receive the kingdom and possess the kingdom for ever and ever.' As the Psalmist says (v. 4), 'For the Lord takes pleasure in his people; he adorns the humble with victory.'

God's 'holy ones' are, of course, his saints – the word is the same. But the saints in scripture are not the special people singled out as holier than the rest of their brothers and sisters: they are the whole community, chosen by God to be 'set apart' from the nations of the earth. The writer of the Epistle to the Ephesians – probably a disciple of Paul – knew this well. According to him, the destiny of the nation of Israel, who were undoubtedly chosen by God to be his 'holy ones', was now to be the destiny of the whole human race, for in Christ, God had made known his desire that non-Jews were also blessed and brought into covenant relationship with him.

The message of Jesus as it is set out by St Luke makes it more specific. Luke is concerned for the outsider and the outcast; in his version of the gospel story Jesus calls the outcast into a life of friendship with God that knows no boundaries and which brings about a change of life and attitude. The standards of normal human and earthly assumptions are turned around. Where the rich are considered of most value; where the over-satisfaction of appetites is thought to be the highest goal of human striving; where laughter and 'looking on the bright side' are the only homely advice that conventional wisdom can offer; and where the all-important factor in what is worth doing is whether it will look good on your c.v. – Jesus comes along and says, 'On the contrary: poverty is a closer indicator of value with God; hunger is preferable to the indulgence that is generally regarded as deserving of worth; to weep and to mourn are surer ways of knowing the presence of God; and persecution and reviling are better than the accolades of a culture whose values are jaded, censorious and exclusive. The only way to live is to love – even your enemies; the only way to find meaning and retain some sense of human worth is to ignore the condemnation of those who would despise you for your simple life-style and your refusal to be bludgeoned into following the latest fashion – even when it is a religious one.'

111

Christians – and other holy people – who have followed this way have never been popular, nor have they ever been easy to live with. But they have pointed to a way of living which most of us aspire to on our best days but shun most of the time; shallowness is so much more comfortable. We give thanks today for those who have had the courage to remind us that there is a better way of living, which does not seem so at the time, but the rewards of which are longer term and infinitely more satisfying.

* * *

The First Sunday of the Kingdom

Isaiah 1:10–18
Psalm 32:1–7
2 Thessalonians 1:1–12
Luke 19:1–10

THE lectionary provides for a 'Kingdom Season' in the final weeks of the liturgical year. The period from All Saints' Day to Advent brings together the themes of All Saints, All Souls, Remembrance Sunday and, in some traditions, the Kingship of Christ. Thus we affirm Christian things about holy people and about dead people within the context of a belief that Christ is King, as we look forward to Advent, which itself looks forward to the coming of Jesus at Christmas.

With savage irony the prophet Isaiah weighs into the city of Jerusalem, comparing it to the cities of Sodom and Gomorrah in Genesis, whose evil was legendary. There is heavy sarcasm in v. 18. The claims to snow-like purity and woollen softness are to be spoken with the kind of intonation that implies, 'Do you really believe this is to be the case?' To complete the passage, the reader needs to continue to vv. 19–20, 'If you are willing and obedient, you shall eat the good of the land; but if you refuse and rebel, you shall be devoured by the sword; for the mouth of the Lord has spoken.' This is no cosy promise to forgive and forget!

Having said that, it is clear that penitence and contrition bring forgiveness and restoration. The Psalmist knew that; even if his

112

experience of impenitence led him to despair. It is this that lies at the root of biblical condemnations to judgment. Those who know the will of God and who fail to observe it are those who stand in greater danger of eternal loss than those who never knew themselves to be numbered among the people of God.

Such is the burden of the message of the opening chapter of 2 Thessalonians. This may have been written by a disciple of Paul in order to 'correct' those who said that the kingdom of God had already come and therefore to urge a more patient and world-affirming life of holiness. Judgment will come, but in God's good time.

The story of Zacchaeus paints a picture of response to and delight in acceptance and forgiveness. It is worth noting several features of the story: first, the nature of the man – small in stature, limited in perspective and petty in aspiration. Second, the initiative of Jesus – it is he who looks up and invites himself to eat with this collaborator, cheat and outsider. Third, the point of the story – the whole reason for the coming of Jesus is 'to seek and to save the lost'. And Zacchaeus can almost be seen to grow taller as he is restored again as an upright son of Abraham.

Such is the nature of God's free and unconditional love. Just as Jesus, he moves out in pity – even for the pitiless – and widens the horizons of the greedy; not so that they will take yet more, but so that they become able to give.

* * *

The Second Sunday of the Kingdom

Job 19:23–27a
Psalm 17:1–9
2 Thessalonians 2:1–5, 13–17
Luke 20:27–38

TODAY'S readings are all about disputes: Job with God, the Psalmist with his enemies, 2 Thessalonians with those who say that the return of Jesus has already happened, and Jesus with the Sadducees.

The passage from the Book of Job is about vindication. Job insists that there exists somewhere the person who will act as his redeemer, in the technical sense of the person in Jewish law who would come to his side and stand to take responsibility for him – as did Boaz for Ruth in her widowhood. 'In the end of the day,' he says, 'the goodness of my life will be apparent, and I will be clear that I have suffered unjustly.' The theme continues in the Psalm, with the Psalmist justly insisting on his righteousness and pleading for God to listen to his pleas and show his love. The writer's enemies are hemming him in, and he needs God to demonstrate the justice of his cause.

The reading from 2 Thessalonians continues with the writer appearing to insist, in the face of those who maintain that the final coming of the Lord has already taken place, that the 'second coming' will not happen until there has been a general period of lawlessness. He thanks God for the faith and faithfulness of the Christians in Thessalonica and reminds them that they are called to 'obtain glory' when the Lord does eventually return. Therefore they are to 'stand firm and hold fast to the traditions that [they] were taught'. Such language suggests that this is someone writing after Paul's time, for he clearly thought that the Lord's coming was imminent, and it seems more likely that one of his followers, rather than the apostle himself, would want to take the disciples back to a tradition of teaching, rather than point them forward to the new direction in which the Spirit was leading.

The Gospel passage has Jesus in dispute with the Sadducees, the group who, we are told, denied any belief in the resurrection. Their trick question is about life 'in the resurrection', and Jesus answers them by taking to task the crudity of their expectations. Resurrection life is not a matter of who belongs to whom; it is about life in the spirit, where the knowledge of God makes possible relationships which transcend normal earthly categories.

What are we to make of these conflicts today, when the opponents of the biblical writers seem to have right on their side? Frequently,

114

now, 'crudity' is to be seen on the part of believers! Many would say that we need to interpret a belief in a literal 'second coming' in the light of (a) what we know about the background to such beliefs in the earliest years of the church's life and (b) of two millennia of Christian history and theology which inevitably have removed any sense of imminence from faith. The future, for Christian people, symbolizes immediacy of the kingdom of God which is always ahead of us. To insist on its literal coming at some indeterminate point in the future is to deny the daily demands of faith, and to deny the validity of the metaphor is to abandon any grounds for hope in the future.

★   ★   ★

The Third Sunday of the Kingdom

Malachi 4:1–2a
Psalm 98
2 Thessalonians 3:6–13
Luke 21:5–19

JUDGMENT is the theme of the reading from Malachi, along with a promise of restoration for those who 'revere God's name'. The Psalmist sings songs of God's victory and the vindication of his people, hence all creation must sing with him.

2 Thessalonians continues the theme of the Lord not returning yet. 'Idlers' probably think that, since the Lord has returned, they do not need to do anything – even work to earn a living. Paul – or the person writing in Paul's name – reminds them of his conduct among them as a non-stipendiary apostle, who earned his own living while preaching the gospel, so as not to be a financial burden to them, and so as to provide them with an example. The lesson is one against sentimentalism; a vibrant faith in Christ leads, not to indolence and a dreamy assumption that other people will support our religiosity, but to a commitment to life, work and the pursuit of a holiness that is rooted in earthly realities.

The reading from Luke comes at the start of the lengthy speech of Jesus which each of the Synoptic Evangelists has during the Lord's last days in Jerusalem. Following the story of the widow's mite, the conversation turns to the beauty of the Temple, and Jesus predicts its downfall. When asked when this is to happen, he warns his disciples against too hasty an assumption that the coming of God's kingdom will be subject to any particular individual's claims. All sorts of other things are to happen first.

The consistent theme here is that of living in the world in the light of the world to come, but with no unhealthy obsession with piety or religiosity. Faith is to be rooted in the here and now; the future, precisely because it is in God's hands, can take care of itself. Such a view stands in stark contrast with those other-worldly approaches to believing which take no account of how life is to be lived, and which set a higher store on thinking the right things and having the right experiences than on living a righteous life.

The whole point of Christian existence in the world is the pursuit of human holiness. Those who 'revere God's name' are those who keep his commandments. Jesus also said, 'Not everyone who says to me, "Lord, Lord," will enter the kingdom of heaven, but only the one who does the will of my Father in heaven.'

*   *   *

The Fourth Sunday of the Kingdom

Jeremiah 23:1–6
Psalm 46
Colossians 1:11–20
Luke 23:33–43

A number of themes are present on this last Sunday before Advent: the Feast of Christ the King; the implications of the kingdom for all earthly rule; and the traditional 'Sunday next before Advent', or 'Stir up Sunday', in Anglican piety.

Shepherds are kings, the rulers of God's people. So the message is to those who exercise authority over others – in whatever context, not just in the Church; for the effect of Jesus is to make the spiritual tradition of the children of Israel applicable to all nations and people. God promises to take care himself for those whom the politicians forget; he expects rulers to rule with compassion. Hence the Psalmist's conviction, 'God is our refuge and strength, a very present help in trouble' for those who have no other access to power, influence and control, even over their own lives. The question is, what is the evidence for this: What are such statements worth in the real terms of contemporary discourse?

An answer is provided from the letter to the Colossians, and it is Christ and the Church. The Church is not sent against the world, but is part of it, praying for it, longing for its contemporary and immediate salvation, and trusting that God will soon come and vindicate those who need comfort and advocacy amid the ruthlessness that determines public life, which forgets the poor and the excluded. The Church's function is to be human, in imitation of Christ, on behalf and in anticipation of a humanity that still awaits its salvation and wholeness in Christ.

In a sense it is remarkable − though in another sense not so − that all this talk of 'kingdom' brings the reader to Calvary. The kind of divine kingship that is conveyed in the total life of Jesus is one of love and sacrifice. The sacrifice of Jesus is a forgiving act (see v. 34: 'Father, forgive'), and the penitent thief stands for all who turn, at whatever end or whatever extremity, to the God who is the Father of Jesus; both the response and the promised healing are immediate in the 'Today ...' of Jesus' answer.

Such kingship is worlds away from the need to control and the conviction of superiority that usually afflicts leaders. What might it mean for those of us who exercise leadership in the Church, the State, or in any community or group to follow such a leadership style? We might seek to draw out the best of discipleship and love; we might give up controlling and instead seek ways of setting others free to explore who they are and what they might become, by the grace of God; we might deny ourselves the glory of accolades from other people and delight only in the joy of those we lead and serve.

117

As we stir our Christmas puddings, we might pray for the Spirit of God to stir up our lives to take seriously the call to love and serve on behalf of him who 'came not to be served, but to serve, and to give his life as a ransom for many'.

Biblical References

120

121

Subject Index

123

Table of First Sunday after Trinity dates and Propers

YEAR	SUNDAY CYCLE	FIRST SUNDAY AFTER TRINITY	PROPER
1998	C	14 June	6
1999	A	6 June	5
2000	B	25 June	7
2001	C	17 June	6
2002	A	2 June	4
2003	B	22 June	7
2004	C	13 June	6
2005	A	29 May	4
2006	B	18 June	6
2007	C	10 June	5
2008	A	25 May	(3)*
2009	B	14 June	6
2010	C	6 June	5
2011	A	26 June	8
2012	B	10 June	5
2013	C	2 June	4
2014	A	22 June	7
2015	B	7 June	5
2016	C	29 May	4
2017	A	18 June	6
2018	B	3 June	4
2019	C	23 June	7
2020	A	14 June	6

* *For Proper 3 use Second Sunday before Lent, Option B (8th Sunday after Epiphany)*

Also published by Canterbury Press Norwich

Exciting Holiness

BROTHER TRISTAM SSF

**Collects and Readings for the Festivals and
Lesser Festivals of the Church of England**

A comprehensive resource for public worship
on the 233 festival and commemorative days
in the new calendar authorized for use
from Advent Sunday 1997.

Contains brief biographies, the collect for the
day, Old and New Testament readings printed
out in full, the Psalm or canticle, the Gospel
reading in full, the post-communion prayer and
sentences. New Revised Standard Version
Bible text used throughout.

ISBN 1-85311-174-0

576pp.   size:185 x 123 mm
Hardback with ribbon marker   £17.99

Also published by Canterbury Press Norwich

Leading Intercessions

RAYMOND CHAPMAN

**Prayers for Sundays, Holy Days and Festivals
- Years A, B and C**

A new collection of intercessary prayers based on
the three-year cycle of the new lectionary.
The prayers are arranged in the customary fivefold
division of subjects - the Church, the world, the
community, the sick and the departed - for use in
public prayer at the Eucharist and at other times.

ISBN 1-85311-176-7

160pp.   size: 198 x 126 mm
Hardback with ribbon marker   £9.99

Also published by Canterbury Press Norwich

Sing His Glory

Hymns for the New Lectionary - Years A, B and C

This practical and comprehensive handbook offers suggestions
for hymns which are linked to the readings for every Sunday,
principal holy day and major festival in the years A, B and C.
Tabulated for easy reference, listings are given for all the
hymn books in popular use: *Hymns A & M, New English Hymnal,
Hymns for Today's Church, Hymns Old and New, Mission Praise,
Baptist Praise and Worship* and others. A wide choice of fitting
music to suit all tastes is offered for each reading - Old Testament,
Psalm, Epistle and Gospel. A unique and vital resource for clergy,
musicians and all involved in planning or leading worship.

Compiled by a panel of cathedral and church musicians appointed
by the Presentors' Conference and comprising Alan Dunstan (Truro
Cathedral), Paul Ferguson (York Minster), Christopher Idle (Diss,
Norwich), Alan Luff (previously of Birmingham Cathedral) and
Charles Stewart (Winchester Cathedral).

ISBN 1-85311-175-9

208pp.   size: 210 x 148 mm
paperback   £8.99